Gallé

Emile Gallé, *c.* 1875. (Private Collection)

EMILE GALLÉ

PHILIPPE GARNER

ACADEMY EDITIONS · LONDON

ACKNOWLEDGEMENTS

I would like to thank the private collectors and institutions who have allowed items from their collections to be reproduced and the many people who have helped me in the preparation of this book including: Lady Jane Abdy, Victor Arwas, Sheldon Barr, Martin Battersby, Linda Baxter-Groves, Bethnal Green Museum, Maria de Beyrie, Sir Eric Berthoud, Maître Georges Blache, Jean Bourgogne, Maria Branca, Amiel Brown, Jean-Claude Brugnot, F. T. Charpentier, Messrs Christie, Manson & Wood, Julia Clarke, John Culme, Richard Dennis, Noëlle Garner, Le Duc de Gramont, Knut Gunther, Margaret Harris, Jeanette Kinch, Alain Lesieutre, Sydney and Frances Lewis, Nourhan Manoukian, Felix Marcilhac, Musée de l'Ecole de Nancy, Musée des Arts Décoratifs, Ferdinand Neess, William Paxton, France Robert, John Scott, Messrs Sotheby & Co., Sotheby's Belgravia, Simon Standish-Kentish, Laurent Sully Jaulmes, Lynne Thornton, Robert Walker, Antonia Wilson-Clarke, Caroline Wilson-Clarke. I would also like to thank Howard Grey for his photographs.

First published in Great Britain in 1976 by
Academy Editions 7 Holland Street London W8

ISBN Cloth 85670 129 7   Paper 85670 416 4

First paperback edition 1979

Designed by Richard Kelly

Printed and bound in Great Britain by
Balding & Mansell Ltd., Wisbech

'Je n'ai point d'autre affaire ici-bas que d'aimer'   Victor Hugo

Inscription on a *vase de tristesse* engraved with the title *Le Sens de la Vie* and dedicated by Emile Gallé to his friend Edmond Rostand

Les Roses de France, c. 1900. (Contemporary engraving)

Contents

List of Colour Plates

Introduction

Statue of Duke Stanislas Leczinsky, Place Stanislas, Nancy.

Carved signature, detail from a firescreen, 1900. (Bethnal Green Museum)

In 1488 the Duke of Anjou issued a special edict granting the privilege for the opening of four glassmaking workshops in Lorraine. This date, and this royal gesture, mark the beginnings of what was gradually to develop into a strong local tradition of glass production. By the 1560s virtually every village in the province of Lorraine boasted its own glass works, and local production was acquiring a reputation that went far beyond national borders. One glassmaker, indeed, Balthazar de Hennezel, complied on several occasions with requests from England to send workmen who could teach their skills to the British.

A formal identity was given to this local craft when in 1601 various firms united, forming a strong co-operative group under the impetus of which the industry thrived, though not without periodic lapses, through the seventeenth and eighteenth centuries.

A key event in the cultural evolution of Lorraine was the abdication in 1735 of Duke Stanislas Leczinsky from the throne of Poland. For the town elected by the Duke as the setting for his retirement was Nancy, heart and capital of the province and, by all accounts, the arrival of so cultivated a figurehead bestowed an altogether more sophisticated mood on the town. The critic Claude Roger-Marx, discussing in 1911 the resurgence of interest in the arts which occurred in Nancy in the last quarter of the nineteenth century is in no way surprised to observe such a renaissance in a town like Nancy, which had retained something of the atmosphere and elegance of a luxurious eighteenth-century capital with its tradition of artistic patronage.[1]

The English magazine *The Studio* published, in 1903[2], a survey in which the critic Henri Frantz reminds us, rather grandiosely, that Nancy is '. . . a city, the refinement of which recalls, on a small scale, that of Athens'. 'It must not be forgotten,' he states, 'that in the eighteenth century Nancy was a remarkably beautiful, indeed a brilliant city, with its rows of imposing edifices, their façades adorned in a style both severe and pure, their entrance gates of finely chiselled ironwork, every detail thoroughly appropriate and harmonious . . .' He goes on to scatter the names of a few great artists whose talents have shone on the town— Claude Lorrain, Jean Lamour and René Moreau.

In the year 1844 a new citizen was attracted to this town. The young man, the son of a highly respected family from Clermont-sur-Oise, arrived in Nancy armed with little more than a classical education, a certain flair as a draughtsman, and a lively and ambitious character. Here he settled to pursue his as yet imprecise aspirations for a career in business. With a strongly developed sense of priorities the young man soon found himself a wife, Mademoiselle Reinemer, a woman born of old Protestant stock and imbued with a deep religious conviction; and it was in the circumstances of his marriage that the seed of his future career was sown. The young man's name was Charles Gallé and his wife was the

Decorative ironwork by Jean Lamour, 1752-56, Place Stanislas, Nancy.

daughter of a Nancy mirror manufacturer.

Charles saw in the Reinemer family business full opportunity for expansion and he applied himself with unbridled enthusiasm to his new-found metier. A first idea that occurred to him was to branch out and add table glassware to the stock. Wishing to avoid the mundane patterns that were the stable production of so many glassworks, Charles set himself the task of developing new designs. Plant life provided the inspiration which he needed, and he commissioned the glassworks of Saint-Denis and Pantin to produce tableware of naturalistic inspiration. Carafe handles or glass stems were modelled after the forms of plant stems, pouring spouts undulated as gracefully as petals. Charles would sketch out decorative floral motifs which were engraved, following his designs, by his own employees in an engraving workshop set up on the Gallé-Reinemer premises in Nancy. Finally, to add colour to the glass, Charles employed the still rudimentary enamelling techniques of Bohemian glass, enamelled after firing. There can be little doubt that this venture proved a great success, for the Emperor himself adopted Charles Gallé's glassware for domestic use at his residences in Biarritz, Saint Cloud and Compiègne.

Encouraged by such a success, Charles Gallé felt confident enough to explore new fields. He was aware that the quality of the glazed pottery produced in the nearby town of Saint-Clément was of a depressingly low standard. The Faïencerie Lorraine de Saint-Clément was resting on its laurels and standards had been allowed to slip. Charles was aware, however, that there survived many of the old moulds that had been used in the eighteenth century. Neglected, and in many cases damaged, these old moulds could, nonetheless, be salvaged, and with them the reputation of the Saint-Clément works.

Charles Louis Edouard Gallé, 1860s. (Private collection)

The Gallé-Reinemer family extended operations, setting up workshops at Saint-Clément, and began production of decorated pottery. The output consisted largely of decorative tableware, and the style was still almost exclusively rooted in the eighteenth century. The Lorraine archaeologist Cayon designed decorative heraldic motifs with a Louis XV flourish which were followed by the artists in the atelier as they applied their brushes to the clay. Charles was able to claim a second success. While her husband employed his time extending the business which she had brought, almost as a dowry, Madame Gallé-Reinemer's time was consumed in bringing up the son, Charles Martin Emile, born to the couple on 4 May 1846.

Biography

The life style of the Gallé-Reinemer household was simple to the point of austerity. Emile was brought up very firmly in the Protestant tradition. Evenings at home would be spent reading the Bible under his mother's auspices, though from an early age Emile's intellectual curiosity added other material to his reading lists. He became a passionate student of poetry, and his rich imagination delighted in thumbing through folios of the work of the Nancy-born artist Grandville, a graphic La Fontaine, whose influence can be traced in Emile's later tendency to give an almost human quality to animals, even to plants.

At school, he was a hard-working student though in later life he could afford to criticise his, in some respects, inadequate education, recording that he had never had any teaching that was of direct help to him in starting his career.[1] The chief criticism which he levelled in later years at his education was that students of his generation leaving college to become 'ouvriers d'art' were never sufficiently equipped to apply their artistry to the dictates of production. He compared his own entry into his chosen career with throwing a dog into water to teach it to swim.

Emile was, perhaps, being ungrateful, for the education which he underwent was one carefully considered by a father well aware that his son would be more enriched by a formal, broad-based education than by a technical apprenticeship. At the local lycée in *seconde* and in *rhétorique* (roughly equivalent to our secondary fourth and fifth years), Emile had two excellent humanist teachers in the persons of Messieurs Duchesne and Hemardinger. These two tutors inspired a deep interest as they introduced their receptive pupil to the masterpieces of French and of Latin literature. Emile displayed an unusual literary talent and, at one point, seemed destined for a professorial career. In *seconde*, in *rhétorique* and in *philosophie* (roughly equivalent to our sixth year) Emile carried off the school prizes for narrative and discursive ability in both French and Latin. Relief from academic studies came with drawing lessons and with long hours of leisure spent visiting the gardens of members of his family already imbued with a devotion to plants. This was to be Emile's salvation. '*Heureusement, l'amour de la fleur régnait dans ma famille: e'était une passion héréditaire. Ce fut le salut*'.[2] Emile enrolled two years running in *philosophie*, and it was at this stage that his passion for natural science became fully aroused. He was fortunate in having as a teacher Professor D. A. Godron, author of *La Flore Française*, and *La Flore Lorraine*. Emile's interest in botany gave a purpose to what had been merely a half-hearted interest in drawing, and he used pencil, ink and watercolour to document animals, insects and plants.

It was at this stage that he made his first contributions to the family business, creating the floral compositions which his father used for the decoration of his glassware and pottery. Leaving the Lycée de Nancy at sixteen, Emile Gallé

Emile Gallé, 1867. (Private Collection)

15

Enamelled glass scent bottles, 1880s. (Sotheby & Co.)

went to Germany to pursue his studies. For four years from 1862 to 1866, mostly at Weimar under the tutorship of a Professor Jade, he devoted his time to a more mature, a more personal form of study. He sculpted and drew, studied plant and animal life in greater depth and also found time to discuss philosophy and listen to the musical works of new composers like Franz Liszt. All the while there grew in him an eagerness to face the more practical problems which he would inevitably encounter if he were to enter the family business, as he clearly seemed destined to do. And so, in 1866, he arrived in Meisenthal in the Saar valley where he enlisted in the celebrated glassworks Burgun, Schwerer & Co. under the direction of Mathieu Burgun. Here he devoted himself to serious and intensive studies of the chemistry of glass.

His talents were already being noticed and admired. In April 1867, a letter to Roger Marx, the critic, from a close friend emphasized Gallé's abilities and prophesied his future success, for unlike Baccarat who merely employed good workmen, Gallé, he remarked, was a real artist and one who, through his combination of good taste and thorough knowledge of botany, could revolutionize the decorative arts.[3]

By 1870 he was back in Saint-Clément and we find him at this date designing faïence tableware in rustic style decorated with witty sketches of cats, dogs, cocks, hens or geese. These services, known as *Services de ferme*, mark the first joint venture between Emile Gallé and the young *Nancéien* Victor Prouvé, who was to become so closely involved both in Gallé's work and with his family in

Foreground
L'Oignon vase, deeply carved cased glass, engraved *'Gallé Expo 1900'*. (Private Collection, London)

Background
Marqueterie sur verre vases, *c.* 1900. (Private Collection, London)

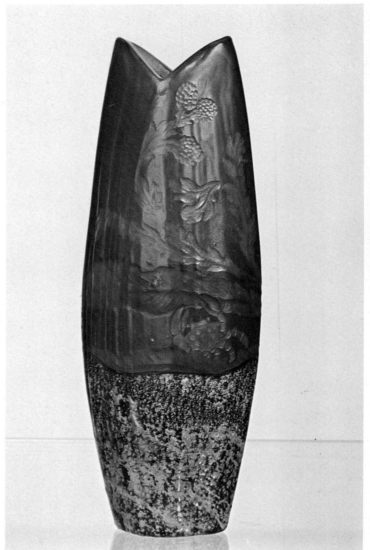

Glass vase with internal decoration, 1880s.
(Private Collection, London). Engraved:

Un jour un certain levrier,
Vit un os de belle apparence
Sans se faire beaucoup prier
Sur ce butin vite il s'élance

Je suis bien dur, dit l'os chagrin,
Car il se plaisait fort à terre.
Sois tranquille, lui dit le chien,
J'ai le temps, je n'ai rien à faire.
Henriette Gallé. E. Gallé fect.
Nanceiis.

Left
Gilt and enamelled Chinoiserie glass vase,
c. 1890. (Private Collection)

Right
Marine vase, intaglio carved and with metallic
foil inclusions, 1890s. (Collection Mr. and
Mrs. Robert Walker)

Left
Scent flacon, carved glass with applied *'Rose
de France'* decoration, *c.* 1900. (Private
Collection, Frankfurt)

Right
Free-form marbled glass vase with carved
decoration, *c.* 1900. (Sotheby's Belgravia)

later years. Victor was introduced to Emile by his father, Gencoult Prouvé. One can imagine the pleasure felt by Prouvé *père* when he introduced his own son to the son of his employer. A lifelong friendship was sealed as they worked together on the decoration of the Saint-Clément faïence. The surprising fact is that Victor was able to make any sort of contribution, for he was only eleven years old. Gencoult Prouvé, a man of unusual inventiveness and imagination, and an energetic worker, became involved with the Gallé family when it fell to him to repair the old moulds in the Saint-Clément pottery. Very soon, he was taking an active part in the creation of new moulds, and Charles Gallé was happy to exploit this fertile and romantic inventor of forms and of decorations. Prouvé *père* was responsible for enlivening the heraldic lions, their forepaws clasping turrets and decorated in blue and gold, which were among the most popular products of the Saint-Clément works. Prouvé's work was always more lively than that of the rather staid Cayon, and his romanticism, often flavoured with a taste for mediaevalism, made a definite impression on the young Gallé. Louis de Fourcaud, Gallé's friend and commentator, notes that even in work exhibited in 1884, there can still be seen the signs of this eccentric collaborator.

Emile Gallé was twenty-four years old when, on 15 July 1870, war was declared between France and Prussia. With hindsight, this war seems to have been inevitable, for ever since their encounter at Biarritz in 1865—at which Bismarck was, perhaps, entertained with the service the Emperor had ordered from the Saint-Clément works—Napoleon III had viewed the growth of Prussian power with increasing hostility. And Bismarck, confident in his success over Austria and thwarted by French diplomacy in his efforts to place a German prince on the Spanish throne, had come to consider a war against France to be vital for the interests of Prussian supremacy. Gallé joined the army as a volunteer in the *23ème Régiment d'Infanterie de Ligne*. Though the effects of the war were to be long-lasting, the fighting was very soon over. Maréchal Bazaine and the army of Lorraine were defeated at Spicheren on 6 August. On 28 January 1871 an armistice was signed after the siege and surrender of Paris and on 1 March 1871 the Treaty of Versailles was ratified. Bismarck levied a heavy indemnity on the French, though this was a burden they were able to bear. He made one very serious mistake, however, in a demand which will be of particular relevance to this study. Bismarck was not fully aware of the deep bitterness that he was to engender by his demand for the annexation to Germany of the provinces of Alsace and Lorraine.

This sad war over and himself demobilized, Gallé was free to continue his experiments and researches. Not quite as free as before, however, for the outcome of the war had cut him off from his friends and from his base of operations at Meisenthal, henceforth occupied by the Germans. Still unsettled after the war Emile Gallé decided to travel to London with his father, who was involved, in 1871, with an exhibition The Arts of France, organised by a Monsieur Du Sommerard in London, and spent a fruitful period of study at the South Kensington Museum and in the Botanical Gardens. On his return to France, Gallé visited Paris and was clearly overwhelmed by the treasures he was able to study in the Galerie d'Apollon of the Musée du Louvre as well as by the work of contemporary craftsmen. In the Louvre he examined the corroded textures and lustres of ancient glassware and was deeply impressed by the techniques and motifs of Islamic enamelled glass, as is shown by the extent of their influence on his own enamelled glass production. The most notable of his contemporaries were Philippe-Joseph Brocard and Eugène Rousseau, the former most admired for his heavily enamelled pieces in Arab taste, the latter for his quasi-oriental glass, characterised by its rich-textured, heavy body, frequently enlivened with a dense, internal crackled effect. When, eventually, Gallé returned to Nancy after travelling in Italy and in Switzerland his eyes had absorbed so many new images that his mind must have reached saturation point. He was bursting to put into practice ideas of his own and to release creatively the knowledge on which he had been feasting and the results of his own experiments.

Back in Nancy after a brief visit to the potteries of Raon L'Etape, Gallé set up his own small but fully equipped glass workshop. At the same time he was evidently putting pressure on his father to re-organise the family business, for between 1873 and 1874 several important changes were made by Gallé *père*, as if in anticipation of his son's inevitable takeover of the family interests. One should remember that Charles Gallé was still providing financial support for his son's intensive studies, for although Emile was contributing designs and collaborating on certain creations, the burden of administering the works still rested entirely on his father. With the sound good sense of his bourgeois background, however, Charles realised that family affairs could only profit from encouraging his son's single-minded interests.

In 1873, perhaps as a symbol of his own success, Charles Gallé had built a large, three storey house named *La Garenne* (The Rabbit Warren), very conventional, very unostentatious in style, yet with an impressive, solid quality. The house, still standing, though its original dense and extensive gardens have vanished, epitomises the background in which Emile Gallé was brought up and from which, as we shall see, he could only escape through the private world of his imagination expressed in an esoteric, veiled manner through the iconography of his personal creations. *La Garenne*, and Emile Gallé's parents, despite his father's artistic leanings, were the embodiment of conservatism, of traditionalist and French bourgeois values. Gallé, whilst outwardly conforming to the tradition set by his parents, was cast in a quite different mould.

Heraldic lion, blue and white decorated faience, *c.* 1870. (Sotheby's Belgravia)

Emile Gallé, 1870. (Private Collection)

Above
La Garenne in the 1890s, viewed from the garden. Gallé's daughters are seated on the grass. (Private Collection)

Left
La Garenne today.

Right
Salon in *La Garenne, c.* 1900. (Private Collection)

Hanging dragonfly lamp in *La Garenne,
c.* 1900. (Photo courtesy Richard Dennis)

Right
Emile Gallé and his wife shortly after their
marriage, 1875, photographed by J. Barche
and L. Gänsch. (Private Collection)

Left
Dining room in *La Garenne, c.* 1900. (Private
Collection)

Charles Gallé provided his son with a workshop and with a studio in the new
family home, and the lush garden became a kind of living library, an invaluable
source of reference for Emile Gallé's botanical studies. Under continued pressure
from his son to move his business, Gallé *père* eventually saw the wisdom of the
idea and moved his Saint-Clément works, both men and materials, to Nancy.
The moment the family interests had been brought together in their home town,
Gallé *père* stepped down as head of the family business, retiring in favour of his
son whom he now judged fully equipped for this responsibility. In the following
year, 1875, Emile Gallé's life struck an uncanny parallel with that of his father.
Charles Gallé had found himself a wife, almost as if marriage were a necessary
prelude to launching his business career. In his case, in fact, his wife's family
business became his own stepping stone. No sooner were the horizons of Emile's
business career opened than he too found himself a wife in the person of Henriette
Grimm, the daughter of a local pastor and, final coincidence, inheritor of a shop
specialising in the sale of mirrors. But Emile Gallé had no need of such a dowry
and his wife's shop was sold immediately. The couple settled in *La Garenne*,
Gallé devoting long hours to his work, and it is from about this period that one can
trace the evolution of his personal style, passing through various phases where
the influence of other cultures can be discerned, to the crystallisation of his
mature style during the 1890s.

Gallé's first independent practical experiments culminated in the sending

Emile Gallé with two friends, Henri and Marguerite Dannreuter, *c.* 1865-67. (Private Collection)

of a group of objects to the Union Centrale Exhibition of 1878 in Paris. It is here, incidentally, that we become aware of his patriotism, outraged by the aftermath of the Franco-Prussian War. Now for the first time Gallé used the Cross of Lorraine as a motif, incorporated with his own name. This first major showing was a success and helped spread an awareness of his name.

He was very eager to continue his experiments. Yet one might be tempted to describe his manner of making experimental glass as an indulgence, for the costs were very high. He realised that to afford himself the luxury of creating *pièces uniques* to his own standards, he would have to earn a good deal from his factory's commercial production. Throughout his working life from this point Gallé, prosperous but not so rich that he could afford to indulge himself without consideration, worked hard to expand the family glassworks. In 1878 he built new furnaces and decorating workshops in Nancy, only a few hundred yards from

Emile Gallé as a student, *c.* 1870. (Private
Collection)

the site of *La Garenne*. The airy workshops with their lofty windows and spacious
working areas and the tall, slender furnace chimneys rising up from the stepped,
sloping roof remained virtually unchanged until Gallé's death, though the volume
of work handled increased substantially. These new premises included studios
for the sketching of designs and, inevitably, their own flower beds, planted by
Gallé as a permanent and accessible source of inspiration and reference.

In her introduction to the first publication of her late husband's writings in
1908, Madame Gallé justifies the inclusion of large tracts of botanical writing
within the title *Ecrits pour L'Art* on the grounds that if Gallé had brought about
a renaissance of decorative art, it was because he had studied botany both as an
artist and as a scientist.

Emile Gallé's involvement in the study of nature is a key feature in the analysis of his art and must be considered side by side with its evolution. By the time
his new factory was built, Gallé had already expressed his interest in botany in a
number of reviews and studies. These and subsequent writings by Gallé, except
of course where the subject is purely practical, distil a *préciosité* very much in
keeping with the aestheticism of the last decades of the nineteenth century, and
the style creates an immediate feeling of distance by its esotericism. But one
must point out the personal character of Gallé's love of nature. That Gallé was,
in general terms, an escapist, there can be little or no doubt. It was symptomatic
of his era for artists and aesthetes to isolate themselves from reality in worlds
of artifice and fantasy. Des Esseintes, created in 1884 by Joris Karl Huysmans
as the hero of *A Rebours* was the archetypal fugitive in artifice. The English title

of *A Rebours* is *Against Nature*, and it is Gallé's great irony that his escapism was the product not of going against nature in the tradition of so many of his contemporaries, but of confronting and immersing himself totally both emotionally and spiritually in nature.

Ever maintaining his outward image of a good citizen and a *bon bourgeois*, Gallé assumed greater responsibilities and, indeed, came to play a leading part around 1880 in the affairs of the Société Lorraine d'Horticulture, including editing their journal. Meanwhile, he was preparing for his next major Paris showing. In 1884 he sent off a substantial exhibit of pottery and of glass to the eighth exhibition of L'Union Centrale de L'Art Décoratif. His contribution won him a gold medal and a measure of publicity. Paris exhibitions fulfilled the dual role of presenting Gallé's production to the public and at the same time creating opportunities for him to meet the leading figures in Parisian Society. By now his success was assured and the twenty years between 1884 and 1904 were, for Gallé, years of expansion, years of experiment and, above all, years of satisfaction in getting ever closer to his ideal of expressing his personality through his unique designs and superlative craftsmanship.

Within a year he had opened a shop for the sale of his glass in Paris at 12 rue Richer. A number of vases survive with the engraved name *L'Escalier de Cristal* beside the artist's signature. Simultaneously with this venture in Paris, Gallé launched himself into work in a new medium at Nancy. He became fascinated with wood and began work on inlay, furniture and sculpture in wood. The Paris Exhibition of 1889 provided the first showplace for his furniture and the items which he had prepared for this exhibition were of a breathtaking quality and inventiveness. His glasswork added to his triumph at this exhibition, winning for him not only a gold medal but the *Grand Prix* and election to the *Légion d'Honneur*. His new techniques of glassmaking were also shown here for the first time. The public was introduced to his two or three layered cameo glass work, with the industrial production of which his name was to become so closely, yet so inaccurately, linked. Very soon plans were under way for the opening of another shop, this time in Frankfurt.

Gallé's energy and enthusiasm were fired by his success and the 1890s were his most fruitful years, building up to a high point at the Paris Universal Exhibition of 1900. During this time his production expanded to a point where he was employing approximately three hundred men and women in his factory. At the same time, there was no shortage of wealthy patrons, ready with commissions for luxurious *pièces uniques*. Emile Gallé was by now a national hero with a reputation of international proportions and he was able to enjoy the privilege of illustrious commissions such as the *Vase Pasteur*, or the pieces offered to the Imperial Russian family in 1896. The *Vase Pasteur* described briefly by Louis de Fourcaud as a crystal goblet offered to Pasteur by the Ecole Normale Supérieure on the occasion of the seventieth anniversary of his birth (30 April 1893), forms the subject of a revealing account by Gallé of the genesis of a work of art.[4] He evidently considered it a commercially significant work and one which he was flattered to undertake. The city of Paris commissioned urns decorated with pink agate flowers on a background of moss-coloured agate and these pieces, their elaborate mounts executed by the Paris *orfèvre* Falize *père*, were presented on 6 October 1896 to the Tzar Nicolas II of Russia in the Hôtel de Ville.[5] De Fourcaud also illustrates[6] a *verseuse*, *Cathleya*, the bulbous body held in a mount of dense acorn-laden fronds, which was offered to the Tzarina.

Emile Gallé was an essentially private character and, whilst doubtless the businessman in him saw the benefits of such commissions in boosting still further his reputation, these official works, however rich, avoid the subjective and intimate qualities to be found in those objects created by Gallé for himself and a small, close circle of friends and cognoscenti. Doubtless, also, he found deeper satisfaction in the effect he had on his contemporaries in Lorraine and his inti-

Vallin's doors for the Gallé factory *in situ*. (Photo courtesy Richard Dennis)

Oak doors by Eugène Vallin for the Gallé Factory, 1896. (Musée de l'Ecole de Nancy)

mate friends than on the reactions of the general Parisian or international public. Devoted to the idea of giving an identity to local craft, Gallé, during the 1890s, gathered around himself a group of artists, most of them in their thirties, whom he weaned from their imitative work and initiated and educated in an aesthetic derived from a frank confrontation with nature. Auguste Daum (born 1853) turned his family glass factory into a *verrerie d'art* in 1893. Eugène Vallin (born 1856) and Louis Majorelle (born 1859), both trained as cabinet makers in servile imitation of former styles, evolved distinctive and dynamic personal styles under Gallé's guidance. Victor Prouvé (born 1858), Gallé's childhood friend, was an important publicist for the group's ideals in his capacity first as teacher, then as Principal, of the Ecole des Beaux Arts of Nancy. The group acquired a greater sense of unity in 1901 when Gallé created the *Alliance Provinciale des Industries d'Art*. Before long, under the popular title of the Ecole de Nancy, Gallé and his colleagues were exhibiting as a team, earning much praise. Ever close to Gallé's and to his colleagues' hearts was the love of nature. In 1892 he devised a work motto '*Ma racine est au fond des bois*', which four years later was carved by Eugène Vallin into the tall oak doors of Gallé's factory. The Ecole de Nancy flourished even after its founder's death, when Victor Prouvé continued the tradition established by Gallé.

Envelope for Gallé's invitation card to the opening of the Universal Exhibition, Paris 1900. (Private Collection)

A corner of Gallé's *Vitrine des Granges* at the Universal Exhibition, Paris, 1900. (Contemporary photograph)

Right
Gallé's display furnace at the Universal Exhibition, Paris 1900. (Contemporary photograph)

Left
The display room at the Nancy factory, *c.* 1900. (Private Collection)

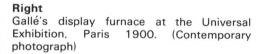

Gallé found a great enthusiast and patron in J. B. Eugène Corbin (1867-1932), founder and publisher of the Nancy-based journal *Art et Industrie*. Deeply impressed by Gallé's work and by the motivation of the Ecole de Nancy, he endeavoured to give them maximum coverage in the pages of his journal. It was for Corbin that Gallé created one of his major works, the surreal mushroom table lamp *Les Coprins*. M. Corbin bequeathed to the town of Nancy virtually his entire collection of Ecole de Nancy works of art. It was left to his daughter, Mademoiselle Jacqueline Corbin, to create the Musée de L'Ecole de Nancy in its present form when, in 1963, she gave the Art Nouveau style family home as a setting for the Museum collection. The name of the *magistrat* Henri Hirsch must feature prominently in any discussion of Gallé's patrons, for it was to celebrate his wedding that the two key pieces of furniture in Gallé's entire oeuvre were commissioned in 1904—the *vitrine aux libellules* and the *lit papillon, Aube et Crépuscule*.

In 1900 Gallé sent out small pamphlets as invitations to the opening, listing his exhibits at the Universal Exhibition, and giving maps and directions. The pamphlets came in envelopes specially printed in watery shades with the sender's name traced in trembling, spidery script. A surprise amongst all the treasures to be seen at the Exhibition, and, surely, even more exciting than the

EMILE GALLÉ

Aube et Crépuscule, 1904. (Musée de l'Ecole
de Nancy)

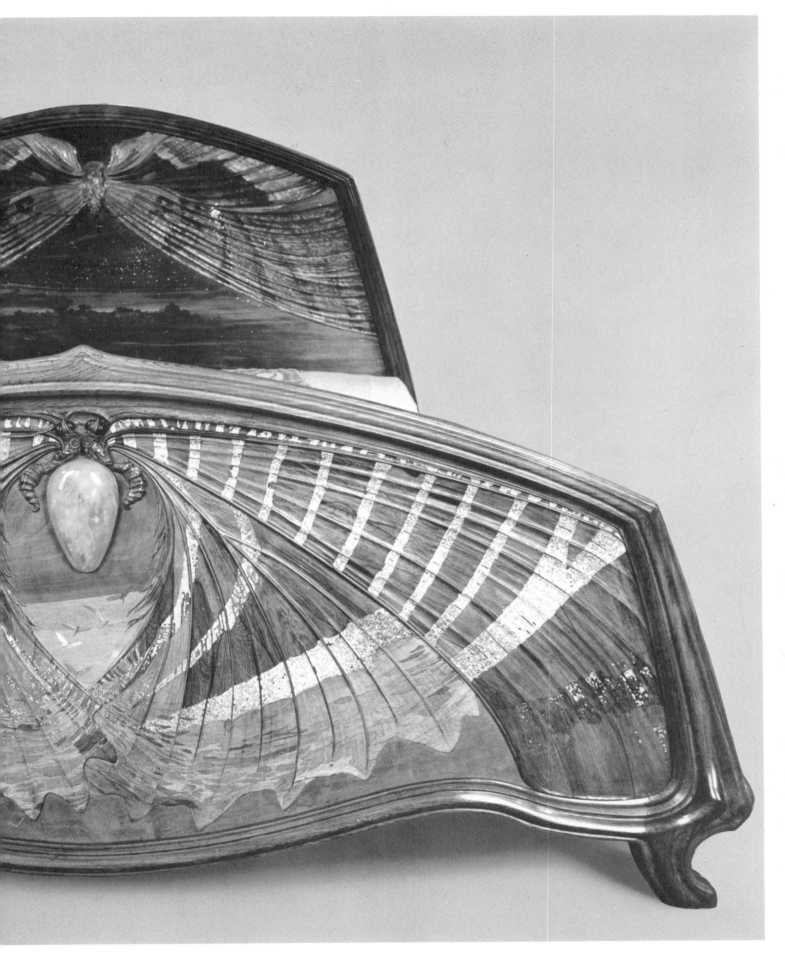

finished objects, must have been the sight of the small glassmaking furnace which Gallé had constructed as the focal point of his display. Here visitors were given a glimpse of the glassmaking process and over the furnace mouth could be read the lines

> *Mais si les hommes sont méchants, faussaires et prévaricateurs,*
> *A moi, les mauvais démons du feu! Eclatent les vases! Croule le four!*
> *Afin que tous apprennent à pratiquer la justice.*

(But if men should be wicked, perverters of truth and justice, come to my help o ye demons of fire. Let vases burst and let the furnaces crumble so that all men learn to be just.)

On the ground lay the hinged wooden moulds into which the molten glass was blown, whilst on shelves and all around were ancient models and vases in various stages of completion. On the ground lay broken fragments of superb vases that had cracked in the making.

Gallé had triumphed. The response was vast and international. A group of items found their way to England after the Exhibition and the Donaldson Bequest of Gallé furniture purchased at the Exhibition forms the nucleus of the Victoria and Albert Museum's collection (now housed at the Bethnal Green Museum), this despite the lament from a critic in *The Artist* (1900) that the French designers were unrealistic and incapable of producing 'one good interior that would be accessible to the well-to-do middle classes.' If exhibition quality pieces proved too costly for any but the wealthy, democratic principles were surely satisfied when in 1904 Gallé opened a shop in London, taking over 13 South Molton Street from the milliner Madame Clematis, to retail commercially produced glassware, putting up a shop sign 'E. Gallé Works of Art', and installing a French manager M. E. Thiroux.

The last few years of Gallé's life had been the years of his greatest triumphs. At home he had found sympathetic and enlightened patronage; in Paris at the Universal Exhibition of 1900 he had scored a huge success with works that attained a high standard of both technical and imaginative inventiveness. His end was near, however, and his sense of impending doom, his awareness that his illness would not leave him many more months of life, inspired a group of *vases maladifs* in which the putrid, sickly colours of the glass, the unhealthy forms and textures reveal their creator's own weakness and debility. On 24 September 1904, he died of leukaemia, leaving a prosperous business to his widow and family. His wife and four daughters continued as always to play a background role; but with two sons-in-law to run the business, with the works manager Emile Lang, and the guidance of Victor Prouvé who now assumed a role as family adviser, there was no reason to let the family name die. The factory continued production until its final closure in 1935, though the glass produced after 1904 shows a marked decline in quality.

A fitting yet unintentional obituary, showing the loss that was felt at the death of their guiding light, was made by René d'Avril in the pages of *Art et Industrie*. In his recollections of the Ecole de Nancy Exhibition of 1904 held in the Galeries de la Salle Poirel, he wrote of *Aube et Crépuscule*: '*Une très particulière émotion s'en dégageait, car Emile Gallé venait de mourir et le magnifique lit de bois incrusté qu'il eut exposé, recouvert d'étoffe violette, décoré de papillons de nuit laissant pleuvoir une impalpable poudre d'or, semblait être l'impressionante couche funèbre du grand ami des insectes et des fleurs.*'[7] (A very special emotion emanated from it, for Emile Gallé had just died and the magnificently inlaid wooden bed, which he would have exhibited, clad in violet cloth and decorated with moths scattering an impalpable golden powder, became the touching funeral couch of the great friend of insects and flowers.)

Gallé's shop at 13, South Molton Street from a contemporary advertisement. (Private Collection)

Aube et Crépuscule, detail, carved opalescent glass, carved fruitwood and mother-of-pearl, 1904. (Musée de l'Ecole de Nancy)

Influences

Detail of black overlaid cameo glass vase, 1890. (Private Collection, London)

Les Roses de France, carved and applied glass, *c.* 1900. (Collection Knut Gunther)

Emile Gallé's involvement with nature was undoubtedly one of the key spiritual experiences of his life. The Gallé family were, by tradition, lovers of plant life, but his interest went far beyond the realms of either academic botanical documentation or sentimental fascination. Love of nature was, for him, a great passion and through his intimate knowledge of plant and insect life he found an escape into a world of the fantastic. His botanical writings, quite apart from displaying a profound knowledge, allow us the occasional aperçu of the power of nature to trigger his imagination. Through his writings one is left with the impression of a man whose mental map of Europe, from the Isle of Wight to Nice or to Northern Italy, is visualised in terms of plants observed or gardens visited.

In 1878 Gallé records the excitement of his visit to the Troubetzkoi Villa at Intra on Lago Maggiore: '..... *Les satisfactions d'ordre purement scientifiques sont ..... accompagnées à la Villa Troubetzkoi par les jouissances les plus vives que puisse goûter un artiste épris d'une nature séduisante, enchanteresse; les étrangers abondent à la villa; ils y sont admis de la façon la plus libérale; une simple carte-de-visite suffit à ouvrir les portes de cet Eden. D'ordinaire, un jardinier conduit les pas du visiteur, en donnant avec exactitude les noms des plantes. J'ai eu la bonne fortune d'être guidé par le prince lui-même... ... Je voudrais pouvoir dire ici toutes les remarques intéressantes, tous les renseignements précieux qui m'ont été donnés par mon hôte pendant une promenade de plusieurs heures à travers six ou huit hectares de plantations de luxe. Chaque objet commande ici l'attention.....*'[1] (At the Villa Troubetzkoi, purely scientific satisfaction is accompanied by the keenest enjoyment offered to an artist enamoured of the charm and enchantment of nature. Strangers abound and are welcomed in the most open fashion. A simple visiting card opens the doors of this Eden. Usually, a gardener leads the visitor on his walk, giving the names of plants with great precision. I was lucky enough to have the Prince himself as my guide. I should like to be able to record all the interesting remarks, all the precious information given me by my host during our walk, which lasted for several hours, through the luxuriously planted six or eight hectares of garden. Each object drew one's attention...)

His sense of wonder on visiting such a garden could be compared with Alice's incredulity in Wonderland. Confronted with Nature, Gallé was immediately divorced from social reality, he was tumbling in his imagination, through literature and through time, always giving an extra dimension to whatever he was observing. Here, he describes a visit in 1878 to the Isola Madre: '*L'Isola Madre, elle, n'est pas une morte dans sa couronne de fleurs, c'est une île véritable et bien vivante. Ce n'est pas néanmoins celle de Robinson; Fénélon plutôt aurait été charmé par ses grottes de fougères et ses bosquets de figuiers. Il aurait placé Calypso dans ses molles prairies, irisées d'anémones, de violettes et de jacinthes.*

37

Certaine plage au sable fin, sous les saules argentés, serait digne d'Ulysse et de Nausicaa. C'est encore Phoebus qui darde ses flèches dans les dessous de bois illuminés ; c'est tout un Olympe qui, là-bas, rayonne à travers une poussière d'ambre et d'or, Olympe aux riches terrasses pavées de citronniers, aux corbeilles glorieuses d'Erythrina et de Salvia splendens. Ces lauriers-roses à fleurs blanches n'évoquent-ils pas les Métamorphoses d'Ovide ?[2] (Isola Madre is not a dead woman in her wreath of flowers, it is a real island, truly alive. It is not, however, Robinson's island. Fénélon would have been the one more likely to be charmed by its grottoes of ferns, its groves of fig trees. He would have set Calypso on its soft meadows, rainbow-hued with anemones, violets and hyacinths. One particular fine, sandy beach, shaded by silver willows, would be worthy of Ulysses and Nausicaa. There, Phoebus still hurls his arrows into the shining undergrowth. Further off, Olympus shines through a haze of gold and amber, an Olympus with rich terraces covered with lemon trees, with glorious beds of Erythrina and Salvia—and flowering laurels with their white blossoms bring to mind Ovid's *Metamorphoses.)*

Using a language rich in sensuality, Gallé personifies flowers. The caress of his words hides depths of meaning one would not expect from the mere inquisitive touch of a botanist. Here Gallé describes the hydrangeas exhibited by Mm

Far left
Flower-form vase with *marqueterie* decoration, *c.* 1900. (Collection Alain Lesieutre)

Left
Glass vase with *marqueterie* and cabochon decoration, *c.* 1900. (Collection Félix Marcilhac, Paris)

Below
Crocus vase with *marqueterie* decoration, silver mount, *c.* 1900. (Private Collection, London)

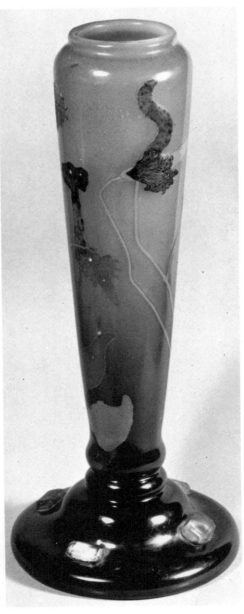

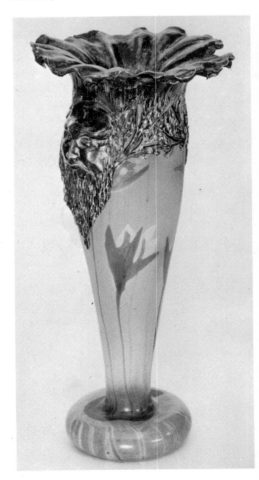

Vergeot and Blaise at the Concours Régional de la Floriculture in 1894: '*Plus loin . . . . . des Hydrangéas étalent la majesté de leurs globes, la fuite de leurs nuances d'une exquise fraîcheur, le turquoise le plus tendre, célestement lavé de pale indigo, neige bleue ou blanche, piquée de boutons de saphir; certains, joliment verdis et blafards, teignent de rose lilacé leur amplitude miraculeuse . . . c'est une détente. Et l'on rend ses sourires à cette nature artificielle qui s'était mise en toilette de garden-party, en robe de soirée de contrat, et qui voulait nous plaire.*'³ (Further in the distance hydrangeas spread out the majesty of their orb-like blossoms and gradations of exquisitely fresh shades—palest turquoise faintly brushed with indigo blue, or snow white dotted with sapphire buds. Some, becomingly green and wan, their marvellous amplitude tinged with lilac pink . . . it is a relaxation. And one smiles at this artificial nature which has put on its garden-party dress, its evening gown, in its desire to please us.)

In another passage he gives character to the rose: '*Mais qui ne préférerait . . . le plus simple bouton de rosier thé, qui, à peine ouvrant l'oeil, déjà semble se pleurer soi-même. Permettez donc à un qui a trop chanté les "plantes molles" d'aimer les roses, et surtout celles qui sont d'avance comme fanées et amoureusement pétries . . . vive la Rose, la reine éternellement adorable!*'⁴ (But who would not prefer . . . the simpler bud of the hybrid rose, which, its eyes barely

Cameo glass vase with prunus blossom decoration, 1890s. (Collection Alain Lesieutre)

open, seems to weep already at its fate. Allow someone who has, for far too long, sung the praises of anaemic plants, to love roses, and especially those roses which start their life with a faded and lovingly moulded look. Long live the rose, the eternally adorable queen.)

The artist's passion for this flower is carried yet further: '*Comment expliquer le pouvoir qu'exercent à la fois, sur les moins nobles et les plus délicats de nos sens, le vertige exhalé par l'odeur des carmins, la flatterie de la nuance, qui s'insinue bien plus avant dans les âmes que la couleur crue ne les blesse, enfin le rêve où, plus subtilement que tout brillant vernissage, nous induit la matité qui veloute sa caresse?*'[5] (How can one explain the power exerted on the least noble and most delicate of our senses by the dizziness of the scent of carmine, by the flattery of subtle colour, burrowing more deeply into our souls than the thrust of crude colour, finally, by the dream-inducing, dusty velvet feel when you touch—more subtle than any shining glaze.)

Finally, by a literary trick of feigned, yet quite deliberate absent-mindedness, Gallé takes the reader into a flight of pure fantasy, on the pretext of describing chrysanthemums and gladioli, before bringing him firmly back to ground with a closing paragraph which makes a fascinating and rare admission. '*Les nôtres glaieuls ont des fleurs (qui).....apportent l'élément du succès des jolies femmes sur les belles.....Elles possèdent ce qui manque à la rose elle-même, le je ne sais quoi, le grain de beauté sous la poudre, beauté du diable parfois... moins fait pour décorer les cultures de plein air que pour ravir d'aise les amateurs.*' He describes the enthusiast, breeding new strains and surprised on studying his creations by '*des similitudes étranges avec des êtres animés; ce sont des phalènes vêtues de crépuscule et d'aurore, des noctuelles ardoisées, des taupins zébrés, des coccinelles tiquetées, les dessins bizarres faits par une goutte d'encre entre les deux feuillets d'un livre, par un miniaturiste arabe dans les vieux corans, des fusions auréolées en plumes de paon, des yeux de poudre sur l'aile des grands Lépidoptères.....Mais, mon cher Lemoine, je m'arrête, vous me diriez que tout cela n'existe que dans mon imagination. Heureusement, le jury les a vues comme moi, ces filles de votre fantaisie...........*'[6] (Our gladioli bear flowers which are a living example of the victory of pretty women over beautiful ones. They possess what the rose lacks, an indefinable quality—the beauty spot under the powder, the '*beauté du diable*' sometimes—less adapted to adorn the great outdoors than to delight the initiated........Strange similarities with living creatures—they are moths, clothed in twilight and dawn, slate-coloured noctuas, zebra-striped spring beetles, speckled ladybirds, like the bizarre drawings made by an inkspot between the pages of a book or by an Arab miniaturist in the old Korans, haloed like peacock feathers, eyes of powder on the wings of the great lepidopteras. But, my dear Lemoine, I must stop or you will tell me that all this exists only in my imagination. Fortunately, the jury saw, as clearly as I did, those daughters of your dream.)

Nature became a part of Emile Gallé's life from a very early age but it was not until his maturity that the individuality of his personal response became manifest. As a child, his introduction to nature was paralleled by his introduction to religion, under the Protestant influence of his mother's side of the family. Nature and religion became and remained two closely linked influences on Gallé's aesthetic. As he grew up, however, and his rich imagination was allowed an ever freer rein, he abandoned the restrictions of Protestantism, evolving a pantheistic attitude to creation. The artist's feeling for the cycle of life and death, for the eternal processes of renewal tied him to nature by the very strongest of bonds. His empathy with creation made him go beyond the limitations of any denominational creed. God is in all things. Nature herself becomes God, and Gallé's devotion to nature acquired a ritualistic quality. His search for the Holy Grail was a search for oneness with nature, a striving for total immersion, which was at once escape and salvation. In his search for self-expression, how-

Enamelled mould-blown glass fish vase, *c.* 1890. (Collection Alain Lesieutre)

Detail of carved glass vase, 1890s. (Collection Alain Lesieutre)

Les Fruits de l'Esprit, 1893. (Contemporary engraving)

ever, Gallé did freely borrow the trappings of Christianity, be it in the traditionally ecclesiastical forms of certain examples of his work, or in their themes, inspired by quotations from the Bible. Yet his artist's mind could never be bound by these borrowings, and there appears at times in his work a dark, almost pagan, Black Mass quality which reflects the very deepest recesses of his own vision of life.

In 1893 Gallé designed a piece of furniture, *Les Fruits de L'Esprit,* on behalf of the parish of Bischwiller as a gift of gratitude to celebrate the fiftieth anniversary in his post of their pastor Daniel Grimm, Gallé's father-in-law. In a manu-

Les Parfums d'Autrefois, 1895. (Contemporary engraving)

Saint Graal et son Tabernacle, 1894. (Contemporary engraving)

script description given to M. Grimm together with the piece of furniture, its creator elaborates on the symbolism of its decoration. Every flower, every bud, every fruit, every tone or texture of wood conceals in esoteric vernacular elements of the message which the gift is intended to make. Gallé clarifies the mystery: '*Les Fruits de L'Esprit, dit Saint Paul, sont la charité, la joie, la paix, la patience, la bonté, la bénignité, la fidélité, la douceur, la tempérance. Et les Fruits de L'Esprit s'épanouissent en une gerbe de fructifications et de symboles, non sur un horizon où le soleil décline, mais sur un ciel d'aube. La charité et la bonté, c'est le blé mystique, et c'est la grappe qui donne le sang symbolique de l'Eucharist. La paix, c'est l'olivier; ses feuilles d'argent se suspendent au bec des colombes, aux entrées des armoires sans défiance. La douceur a pour figure le fruit du figuier généreux, la tempérance celui du dattier. La bénignité, c'est l'abeille bénévole qui récolte pour autrui, la joie, c'est le myrte, c'est le narcisse et la claudie, le printemps dans la nature et le pardon dans les âmes. La fidélité, c'est la fleur de véronique.....*'[7] (The fruits of the spirit, says St. Paul, are charity, joy, peace, patience, goodness, kindness, faithfulness, gentleness and moderation. *Les Fruits de l'Esprit* blossom forth in a sheaf of fecundity and symbol, not against a sunset horizon but against a sky lit by sunrise. The mystic corn is charity and goodness, the grapes symbolize the blood of the Eucharist; the olive tree is peace, its silver leaves hanging from the beaks of meek doves at the cabinet doors. The fruit of the generous fig tree represents gentleness, that of the palm-tree moderation. The benevolent bee, gathering for others, is kindness, the myrtle is joy, the narcissus and dandelion symbol of Spring and of forgiveness in the soul. Veronica is the flower of faithfulness.)

But his most directly religious creation was surely his *Saint Graal et son Tabernacle* of 1894. The cabinet, richly inlaid with marquetry work, has a distinctly ecclesiastical flavour in the attenuated front panel with its trilobe top and in the openwork bronze halo of stylised thorns. Other examples abound; the trilobe motif is repeated in other items of furniture, including the commode *Les Parfums d'Autrefois* of 1895 and a mirrored wardrobe of 1900. Louis de Fourcaud, who was to become the owner of the *Saint Graal et son Tabernacle*, describes this *Graal de Percifal* as a '*royal calice d'ambre doré, empli et baigné d'un sang vermeil, digne des mains d'un Joseph d'Arimathie ou d'un Titurel...*'[8], and he illustrates[9] a glass vase entitled with St. Matthew's words *Heureux les Pacifiques car ils Possèdent la Terre.*

The influence of the Bible on Gallé's work is just one example of the power exerted over him by the written word, and of the extent to which his creations are the embodiment of literary and poetic ideas. Many works in glass or in wood are engraved or inlaid with lines of verse or literary quotations and endeavour to illustrate the words they bear, either in their form or their decoration. Yet the literary character of his work is on far more profound a level than that of occasional illustration, for the use of quotations is little more than a commercially successful conceit, and, undisputably, there are many works of a deeply poetic or anecdotal nature which make no overt literary references. Gallé was not an illustrator, he was a poet using glass and wood instead of words and his aim was to create tangible, or rather tactile, works of art in three dimensions which could be as moving, as evocative and as full of nuances as any poem. Texture, colour and symbol are orchestrated in symphonies, rich in undertones and echoes and with the power to haunt of certain enigmatic melodies. His compositions are built up through layers of disguised allusion achieving a quality of infinite mystery.

Emile Gallé was a very great glassmaker, his technical inventiveness is without parallel and his skills are quite staggering. He developed an equally deep sympathy for wood, learning to exploit the native qualities of rare and exotic fruitwoods in harmonious juxtaposition. Technical mastery was, for him, however, merely a means to an end. Certainly, on the occasion of important exhibi-

Cased glass vase engraved with lines from Victor Hugo *'O forêts, ciel pur, Ombre des grandes chênes, Au delà des haines, Vous cherchez l'azure',* 1890s. (Sotheby & Co.)

tions, business sense encouraged him to execute and vaunt technical tours de force. Thus the admiration inspired, for example, by his *marqueterie sur verre* technique, introduced in 1897, is the result of the difficulties of the process and the high failure rate at the kiln. Surely, this is misplaced admiration, for Gallé would use glass or wood only as a vehicle for expression and he could succeed in arousing the imaginations, the souls of sensitive appreciators as easily in a carved cameo vase as in the most elaborate *marqueterie* or applied glass creation.

Gallé's personal library was extensive. Brought up on the staple diet of Romanticism, he acquired a strong taste for Chateaubriand (how closely his own botanical writings can be compared with Chateaubriand's descriptions of the New World in their lushness and sense of thrill and wonder). Victor Hugo was a firm favourite, especially as the author's political views were so in keeping with those of the Gallé family. Not until after his school days, however, did Gallé read many of those authors who were to have the most profound influence on him. Foremost amongst these was Charles Baudelaire, whose volume of verse *Les Fleurs du Mal* was first published in 1857 and was, for many years, too controversial to be included on school study lists. The Gallé family library includes the 1879 third edition of Baudelaire's *Les Curiosités Esthétiques* and the 1882 edition of *Les Fleurs du Mal* both published by Calmann-Levy. It would seem probable that Gallé's acquaintance with Baudelaire's work dates from about the time of the acquisition of these two volumes. Baudelairean ideas only become apparent in works after this date, and, more significantly, the purchase of these volumes was, apparently, followed by a period of intense familiarisation with their contents. Pages that made a particularly strong impression were marked and annotated.

In a footnote to his *Ecrits pour l'Art* the origin of the Gallé motto 'Ma racine est au fond des bois', is given by the editor as a sentence by Moleschott: 'C'est par les plantes que nous tenons à la terre; elles sont nos racines'.[10] A later commentator[11] is surely more accurate by pinpointing the following passage from Baudelaire's *Curiosités Esthétiques*: 'Les mieux doués.... sont ces voyageurs solitaires qui ont vécu pendant des années au fond des bois.... contemplant, disséquant, écrivant.... ils savent l'admirable, l'immortel, l'inévitable rapport entre la forme et la fonction. Ils ne critiquent pas, ceux-là, ils contemplent, ils étudient.' (Most gifted.... are the solitary travellers who have lived for years in the depths of the woods.... contemplating, dissecting, writing.... they know the admirable, immortal, inevitable relation between form and function. These men do not criticise—they contemplate and study.) The implication of a kind of spiritual communion held in this quotation so closely approximated the, as yet, ill-defined forces that were driving him that, undoubtedly, Gallé must have been struck, and encouraged by the sentiment expressed. The effect of Baudelaire's writings was catalytic. Gallé's own motivations became clearer to him. During the 1880s he entered the period of his own Symbolism, his ideas crystallised by his readings, paying frequent homage to the poet who so inspired him. In 1896 he created a cabinet, *Les Fleurs du Mal*, inlaid with macabre and sinister plant motifs. From 1892 dates a vase inspired by the lines of Baudelaire's *L'Homme et La Mer*:

> Homme, nul n'a sondé le fond de tes abîmes,
> O mer, nul ne connaît tes richesses intimes,
> Tant vous êtes jaloux de garder vos secrets.

Other poets inspired or encouraged him, Maeterlinck, Sully-Prudhomme, Rimbaud, Mallarmé, Verlaine, Gautier, Marceline Desbordes-Valmore and Count Robert de Montesquiou. Gallé's Essay *Le Décor Symbolique*, delivered as a speech in 1900 to the Académie de Stanislas, is his own attempt at explaining the significance of symbolism in his work.

Les Fleurs du Mal, 1896. (Contemporary photograph)

Page 45, above
Snuff bottle, carved glass, engraved on the insect's bared heart *'Mon Coeur Avez'*, the base engraved *'Emile Gallé Nancy, Exposition 1889'*. (Sotheby's Belgravia)

Below
Marine bowl, internally decorated blown glass with carved applications, *c.* 1900. (Collection Félix Marcilhac, Paris)

Page 46, left
Vase Maladif, applied decoration and iridescent surface effects, *c.* 1900-1904. (Collection Mr. and Mrs. Robert Walker)

Right
Les Têtards, cased cameo and applied glass engraved: *'Aux fosses la lentille d'eau de ses feuilles vert-de-grisées étale le glauque rideau'* Théophile Gautier, Expo 1900. (Collection Mr. and Mrs. Robert Walker)

Page 47
Le Lys, free-form blown glass with applied decoration, bronze mounted, 1900. (Private Collection, Paris)

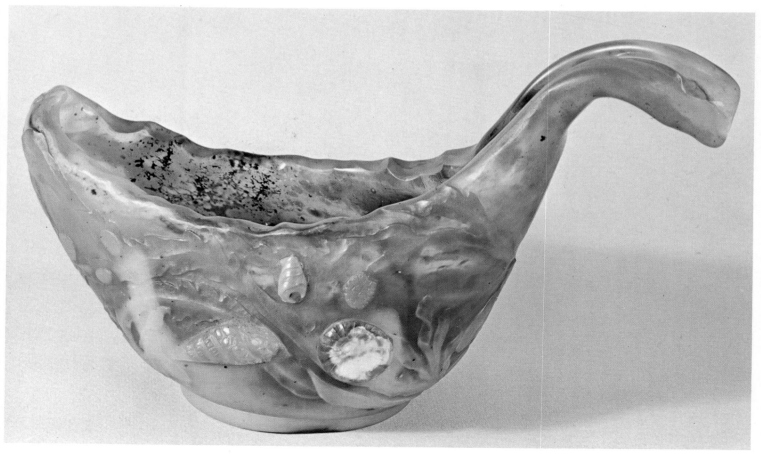

Nous chasserons la Guerre et le Meurtre à Coups d'Ailes, 1890s. (Contemporary engraving)

Trilobe wall bracket, *c.* 1890. (Collection John Scott)

Table lamp, cased cameo glass shade, blown glass stem and wrought-iron base, *c.* 1900. (Collection Félix Marcilhac, Paris)

Pacifism is a theme that recurs periodically in Gallé's work, a theme for which he derives support from the poets. Two vases illustrated by Louis de Fourcaud serve as good examples. Both bear titles borrowed from Victor Hugo: *Plus de guerre, plus de sang*[12], and *Nous chasserons la Guerre et le Meurtre à Coups d'Ailes.*[13] The vase mentioned earlier, *Heureux les Pacifiques, car ils Possèdent la Terre,* must be included within this group, as should the vase, more abstract in its idealism, *Nous monterons enfin vers la Lumière.* Gallé's instinctive pacifism was, however, tinged by the circumstances of the Franco-Prussian War. From 1871 until well after Gallé's death the fires of resentment burned in the hearts of the people of Alsace and Lorraine, and Gallé, in his capacity as a local celebrity, adopted the role of figurehead, of spokesman for the feelings of his compatriots. He expressed the feelings of the people of this lost corner of France in a series of works, with sincerity, with sadness, yet with a fierce sense of local pride.

Louis de Fourcaud describes a curious plate in the collection of Princess Louise of England, Marchioness of Lorne, depicting with naive patriotism the forget-me-not of Alsace withering, nailed to the gallow post of Germany beneath the gaze of an owl and in view of the spires of Strasbourg. The thistle, emblem of the town of Nancy, became a bristling symbol of hostility when coupled, either in wood marquetry or on glassware, with the threatful motto *'qui s'y frotte s'y pique'.* The foremost example of flowers being marshalled by Gallé to represent the feelings of the people of Lorraine is a table designed on the occasion of the

Je Tiens au Coeur de France, detail of stretcher carving.

Below
Carved *'hyalite'* glass vase, 1890s. (Photo courtesy Richard Dennis)

Franco-Russian alliance of 1893 and presented by the people of Lorraine to the Tzar of Russia. It bears the inlaid title *Flore de Lorraine. Gardez les Coeurs qu'avez Gagnés*—keep safe the hearts that you have won—for in an alliance with Russia could be seen the hope of ending the German threat and occupation. The tabletop is a glorious profusion of flowers, each representing one of the towns or villages of Lorraine; the honesty of Lunéville, the wild white rose of Epinal, soapwort of Dombasle and, of course, the thistle of Nancy, among a host of others, each explained by Gallé in a letter to Roger-Marx. Amidst those symbols of the artist's deep-rooted attachment to his native province hope and perhaps optimism burst through as the flowers part to reveal a clear and bright horizon.

His monument to patriotism, however, is surely the large table *Je Tiens au Coeur de France*, which featured at the inauguration of the Exposition Centennale des Beaux-Arts Français in May 1889 and was then sent to the Paris Universal Exhibition of that year. According to Gallé's own description of this piece, in his notes of 11 June 1889, as a *'Table de Musée'*, it is made quite clear that this is a public and not a private work. Carved in walnut and plumwood, the massive table supports an ebony top inlaid in various woods. Within a celtic border designed by Louis Hestaux, a long panel bears and depicts allegorically the lines from Tacitus: *'Germania omnis a Galliis Rheno separatur'*, and its translation *'Le Rhin sépare des Gaules toute la Germanie'*. The figural allegory bears the signature of Victor Prouvé. Grotesques support the table and bear the shield of Lorraine, whilst the stretcher is carved in full relief with thistles intertwined with the legend *'Je Tiens au Coeur de France, Plus me Poignent, plus j'y Tiens'*. The tone is defiant. Branded on the stretcher is the signature *'fait par Emile Gallé de Nancy en bon espoir 1889'*.

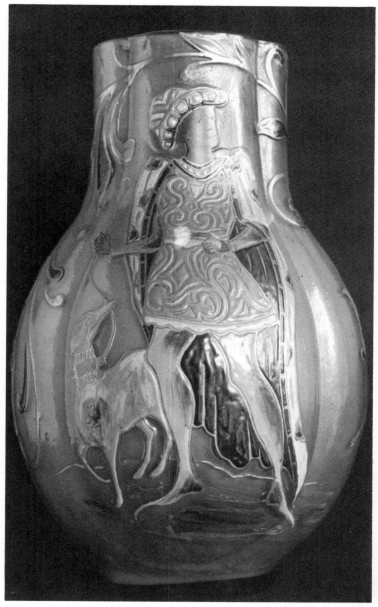

Above
Flacon in mediaeval style, *c.* 1880. (Sotheby & Co.)

Right
Enamelled glass vase in mediaeval style, 1880s. (Collection Alain Lesieutre)

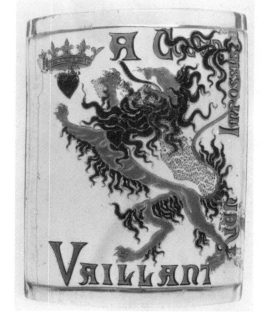

A coeur vaillant rien impossible, enamelled glass plaque with foil inclusions, 1900. (Sotheby's Belgravia)

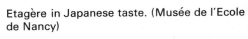

Etagère in Japanese taste. (Musée de l'Ecole de Nancy)

Signature on a glass vase.

Marqueterie sur verre glass vase in Japanese taste, engraved *'étude', c.* 1900. (Collection Alain Lesieutre)

The influences discussed above have all been on Gallé's imaginative force rather than on his style, and, perhaps, it would be unjust to emphasise stylistic influences on the work of an artist for whom content rather than style was the prime focus of interest, an artist whose acknowledged source of inspiration was nature and the natural processes of creation. Nonetheless, Gallé's style was susceptible to outside influences. During his formative years during the 60s and 70s, Gallé had been tempted for a while, first under the influence of Prouvé *père*, and then working in collaboration with Victor Prouvé, by a romantic mediaevalism the influence of which is clearly apparent in his early enamelled glassware and in certain faiences. He expressed his enthusiasm for Venetian, for Renaissance or for Islamic glassware in slavish pastiches which he soon outgrew. He was even, on occasion, tempted to lapse into eighteenth-century traditionalism. This is understandable in certain faiences because of the circumstances under which the Gallé family revived the Saint-Clément works, but it is less excusable in his furniture.

Although such involvements were generally transient, one went deeper and had a lasting effect on his aesthetic—his passion for Japanese art. Feeling deep sympathy for this art of elimination, he assimilated the lessons to be learnt from it, and his works inspired by the influence of Japan were those of a disciple, and not of a pasticheur.

From Japan Gallé learnt a good deal of graphic elegance, and acquired a sensitive appreciation of the skills of abstraction and stylisation whilst remaining

Enamelled glass decanter service in Japanese
taste, *c.* 1890. (Sotheby & Co.)

Internally decorated mould-blown glass vase
1890s. (Collection John Scott)

true to the essence of the object abstracted. He understood the value of the line that limits and explains forms, and came to appreciate the values of close observation. Both the daring use of silhouette and of deliberate asymmetry were lessons taught by Japanese art. It is not certain when Gallé made his first rewarding confrontation with this type of art. It has been suggested that the catalyst was a certain Takacyma, a Japanese student at the Ecole Forestière de Nancy between 1882 and 1885, whose drawings were admired by both Gallé and Eugène Vallin and who undoubtedly exchanged many ideas with the *Nancéiens*. Yet it seems unlikely that this was the first serious encounter. Surely, on his visit to London in 1871, he must have been aware of the enthusiasm for Japanese art among fashionable circles—Whistler and Godwin had already decorated their homes in Japanese taste by 1867, and Rossetti, William Morris, Oscar Wilde and others had become keen advocates after their first major exposure to Japanese wares at the 1862 Exhibition in South Kensington.

Japanese art was the most significant single stylistic influence on Gallé's mature work, both in his feeling for line and in his colour sense, for the delicacy of Japanese colour schemes was frequently reflected in his work. Certain vases bear the inscription *'alla japonica'* beside Gallé's own signature and, on occasion, rather than interpret Japanese ideals within the context of his own imagery, he would acknowledge his debt by the respectful homage of imitation. Henri Frantz, commenting on Gallé's art in 1897[14], is perceptive in his claim that 'It was from Japanese art that he derived the general scheme, the fundamental principle of his style; but we must not infer that he imitates it in any servile manner. Nothing could be more unlike Japanese art than Monsieur Gallé's work.... Only the idea of the Japanese style is also his; and given that principle he has worked it out by the light of his own instinct and taste. He finds constant inspiration, nay, even collaboration, in nature. When Monsieur Emile Gallé reproduces plant form he extracts from it its decorative lines and colouring with the most artistic sense. He seems to condense the whole motive of a plant, to give it an attitude, a movement, to draw out its individuality in a very living way, and yet never to lose sight of the use and end of the object he is designing.'

Above
Vases in *marqueterie sur verre, c.* 1900. (Collection Alain Lesieutre)

Left
Blown glass vase with abstract decoration of Japanese inspiration, *c.* 1900. (Collection Alain Lesieutre)

Right
Carved cameo glass vase, engraved with the line from Maeterlinck: *'Il faut cependant que l'une d'elles commence, pourquoi ne pas oser être celle qui commence . . . .'.* (Collection Alain Lesieutre)

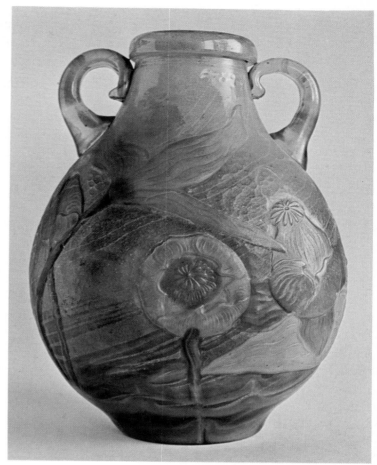

Faience

Underglaze stencilled markings on a faience plate, *c.* 1870. (Photo courtesy Richard Dennis)

Messrs. Lair-Dubreuil and Henri Baudoin, the Paris auctioneers, must have been very excited by the sale which they organised for 13 May 1914. For they were entrusted with the sale of the personal collection of contemporary art of no less a figure than the late Claude Roger-Marx, former *Inspecteur des Beaux-Arts* and great patron of Emile Gallé. The sale included examples of the work of some of the leading artists of the day in porcelain, earthenware, glass, *pâte de verre* and enamels, of names such as Chapelet, Cros, Dammouse, Doat and Rodin. However, it is lot 64 which holds a special interest. The catalogue entry reads: '*Les Nénuphars. Potiche de faïence à couvercle d'émail gris vert. Décor gravé représentant les rides de l'eau; fleurs et boutons de nénuphars avec paillons d'or. Epoque 1884. Haut, 21 cent.*'

This item, knocked down, incidentally, for 165 francs, would seem from the catalogue description to incorporate all the more pleasing qualities of Gallé's faience, exploiting as it does the subtleties of various enamels and glazes and textures, with its carved surface effects and metallic details. And, of course, the choice of decorative motifs is so appealing: the shimmering dragonfly, a creature dear to Gallé, buzzing among lily buds and flowers, all motifs so evocative of the period.

Roger-Marx evidently saw all the virtues of Gallé's creations in faience and, quite apart from a positive display of appreciation by the acquisition of examples for his own collection, he was heard to lament in 1911 the neglect into which this category of Gallé's art had fallen, unjustly neglected by the present generation and yet so worthy of attention. He records how, when visiting old homes in Paris or in the provinces, in Dijon, Blois or Pau, one is quite likely to stumble across items decorated some twenty or thirty years earlier when the Nancy master was giving a modern quality to traditional forms, items endowed with a flavour of individuality, the strength that distinguished the earthenware of days gone by. And he prophesied that the time would come when the charm and wit of these ceramics would again be valued and that they would be as fervently collected in the future as were the products of the Rouen, Moustiers and Nevers schools at the time he was writing.[1]

If Gallé's work in faience has never enjoyed the praise bestowed on his finest creations in glass and wood, it is, quite simply, because he never achieved the same maturity in faience as in the other two media. A critic of 1905 pinpoints this difference when he describes the glass of Gallé as being much more personal than his ceramics.[2] In fact, the more fascinated Gallé became by wood and glass, the less interest he showed in the medium that had served him as a kind of early practice ground. After exhibiting at the Salon du Champ de Mars of 1892, he virtually abandoned his experiments in ceramics.

Brought up in a family of *verriers faïenciers*, Gallé had spent several years

The glassworks at Nancy, marquetry panel, *c.* 1900. (Musée de l'Ecole de Nancy)

Project, in water-colour, for a faience pot, c. 1800. (Photo courtesy Lynne Thornton)

Part-biscuit faience charger, 1800. (Sotheb & Co.)

as an apprentice in his father's works at Saint-Clément learning the basic skills of potting and of decorating. Gencoult Prouvé's enthusiasm fired the young Gallé and, whilst still a student, he provided inventive and humorous ideas for the decoration of faience wares. Here was the germ of so many ideas that were to mushroom later, and here can be observed the birth of Gallé's fascination with the minute, the microcosmic details of plant and of insect life and of his witty personifications and imaginative details. When Gallé took over the family business in 1874, he diverted a high proportion of his creative energy into experiments to widen the scope of the local clay and tin-based glazes which were favoured by a still-lingering tradition.

The culmination of these experiments was in his entries to the Eighth Exhibition of the Union Centrale des Arts Décoratifs in 1884 and to the Universal Exhibition of 1889, which are fortunately well documented by their creator. In favour of a closer analysis of Gallé's ceramic work, Roger-Marx commented that a study of it revealed the development of Gallé's personality and his progress towards the sources which were ultimately to nourish his genius almost exclusively.

The production of faience in Nancy was evidently a commercially successful venture for Emile Gallé and one in which he took a great deal of interest, at least for the first fifteen years, supervising and organising his craftsmen and designers into an effective working team. It is with much pride that he describes the functioning of his factory. Pottery production involved three basic stages: the conception of decorative motifs, experiments with forms and materials, and, finally, the actual production process. Decorative motifs were designed either by Gallé or by his pupils, and usually nature was the theme. Gallé is not being strictly accurate, however, in his claim, made in September 1884, that *'La nature est toujours prise par Gallé comme point de départ et qu'il s'efforce de s'en affranchir à temps pour atteindre le caractère et l'accent personnels'.*[3] (Nature is always Gallé's point of departure. He tries, however, to free himself from it soon enough to give his work its own individual character.) Louis de Fourcaud reminds us that it was not until after 1889 that Gallé abandoned the human figure in decoration. Certain faiences made before this date and bearing overt historical references would also seem to contradict Gallé's claim; de Fourcaud provides the examples of shepherds inspired by Teniers, and *Reiters* or German mercenaries inspired by Callot. Essentially, though, the claim is valid, for in any works in which Gallé was expressing himself and giving rein to his own creative mind it was from nature that he derived inspiration.

Once an idea had been born, with the factory's own gardens as a permanent source of reference, a team of experimenters evolved the most suitable techniques of production in their own laboratory equipped initially with coal and wood firing and then with a *'Système Seger'* gas. Here they worked from maquettes, from watercolour sketches and with sample glazes and enamels evolving the models for commercial production. Gallé describes the factory as being part-mechanised. Motor driven equipment prepared the fireproof clay for making saggars and glaze-melting pots, and for the construction of muffle-furnaces, as well as the pottery clays and enamels themselves. The firing of unglazed bodies and of enamels took place either in the muffle-furnaces or in reverberating furnaces, with the power to throw back the heat. A furnace of a slightly different kind, a high temperature crucible, was used for the melting of enamels and glazes. Gallé proposes three categories for the classification of his production. A first to include *articles de curiosités et d'art*, a second, embracing all *objets de fantaisie* destined for sale commercially, either in France or for export, and a third section for special commission, *Services de Luxe en faïence à émail stannifère.*

Gallé's first experiment with faience involved the intensive exploitation of traditional local clay with tin-based glazes, disdained by many as a crude mat-

Faience vase, autumnal coloured glazes, 1880s. (Sotheby's Belgravia)

Faience sunflower vase, 1880s. (Sotheby's Belgravia)

erial, usually described as *'faïence commune'*. Gallé felt that, however humble this medium, it was still capable of being exploited and enhanced by entirely new methods. Considerable effort was involved in the preparation of enamels and glazes coloured in the mass with metallic oxides, and of a range of colours that brought excitement to the opaque tin-based glazes. Cobalt oxide gave a rich blue, copper oxide a green, whilst other shades were achieved by the admixture of chromium, iron or manganese oxides. Thick, lustrous enamels were contrasted with matt, sparse areas, and opaque with translucent enamels. Occasionally the surface of a piece would be relieved by a bare patch of biscuit clay, its rough, crude texture a most effective foil for the sleek glazes. For small items of more precious appearance, Gallé evolved a whole series of low-fired, tin-based glazes that could be delicately applied with a brush. These fell into two groups, one opaque, derived from a base of oxide of tin, the other translucent, derived from a base of red lead, borax and sand. When ground down and suspended in a fluid the most delicate decorations could be applied by means of a long brush and fired over high-fired base glazes. The 1884 Exhibition also included faiences decorated with carved or textured details and glazes enhanced with the use of metallic foils and inclusions. The latter effects, however, were to be pursued to greater advantage in the years preceding the 1889 Universal Exhibition.

Gallé exhibited some two hundred items of pottery at this Exhibition. Feeling, perhaps, that he had exhausted the possibilities of the plain local clay, he presented for the first time variations on the basic medium. He claimed to have perfected, after lengthy and costly researches, *'une pâte dense, fine, légère, dure, blanche, très sonore, prenant sans défaut l'émail stannifère et les glaçures boraciques plombeuses.'*[4] (a dense, delicate, light, hard, white and very sonorous

Faience heraldic lion, underglaze gilt and decorated, *c.* 1870. (Sotheby & Co.)

Decorated faience plates, *c.* 1880. (Photo courtesy Richard Dennis)

paste which took both tin-based enamels and boracic lead-glazes flawlessly.) These exhibits represent the peak of Gallé's achievement in pottery and incorporate the full range of techniques which he attempted and mastered. By 1889 Gallé had discovered endless ranges of colour for plain tin-based enamels and glazes. He claimed a palette of several hundred shades describing with particular pleasure the gold, enamel, and the beautiful red, black, violet and orange glazes he was now able to achieve. In addition to these plain colours Gallé could boast a range of '*teintes rompues, émaux sablés, picquetés*', delicate speckled effects comparable with the fine graining of a bird's egg; lilac on green, dark brown on light, or other combinations of colour suspended as particles within a semi-opaque glaze, gave the appearance of depth associated with velvets.

Further researches into colour produced a range of enamels with subtle nuances of tone, flawless, strongly adhesive enamels which could be applied in substantial relief and which, in the infinity of shades of pink, purple and lilac were strongly reminiscent of Chinese *famille rose* enamels on porcelain. Translucent enamels were used over metal foils and the effect achieved was comparable with that of Limoges enamels. Contrasts of enamel against biscuit clay were still employed, though with the added subtlety of new tones of clay, for Gallé was now mixing his oxides into the body itself as well as into its skin. Further variations included the superposition of glazes with successive firings. Outer layers of glaze would gather in hollows forming dense areas of colours, whilst the underlying colour would show through the thinly spread areas of relief. To lighten the rather sombre character of stoneware, Gallé suggested treating the surface as a kind of cloisonné, drawing recesses into the soft, unfired body. These could then be filled in, using a brush, with enamels richly coloured with gold, pink, purple or lilac, or with a *matière* derived from iron or from chromium stannate, warm in colour and holding metallic particles in suspension sparkling distinctly within the glaze.

Finally, Gallé included a series of exhibits displaying the various processes of incising, etching or carving decoration which he had evolved. Hydrofluoric acid was used as an etching agent. Gallé describes how the acid would react with

Faience cat, *c.* 1880. (Sotheby's Belgravia)

Faience parakeet pitcher, underglaze gilt and decorated, *c.* 1880. (Collection Alain Lesieutre)

Faience cockerel, *c.* 1880. (Photo courtesy Lynne Thornton)

varying intensity on different clays or surfaces. Quite apart from its application to the creation of relief decoration which could, if so desired, be reserved in contrasting enamels, the acid was used to alter surface texture. Backgrounds matted by the action of the acid accentuated brilliant superimposed decoration, or vice versa. Gallé taught his potters to incise decoration into the unfired, soft clay with a point, or to texture this soft clay with the pattern of impressed wood or of irons. Gilding was sometimes incorporated at this stage in a technique comparable with the gilding of bookbindings, the comparison being Gallé's own. Especially innovative was Gallé's application to faience of the glass carver's and engraver's tools. Fine emery wheels, grinding wheels and diamond points all played a part in extending the possibilities of decorated pottery.

Gallé's *notice d'exposition* of 1889 not only enumerates his technical achievements, it also provides a virtual manifesto of the artist's aesthetic motivations in the medium of faience. Above all, he was anxious to avoid the trite or uninspired; at a time when oriental ceramics were becoming westernised and commercial, he was keen to inject a new vigour into domestic production, giving to each object created a quality of individuality, of technical achievement and of humour. Towards this end he devised his subtle, delicate colour schemes, his unexpected contrasts of bared body and smooth enamel, and he would deliberately leave the signs of handwork, the delightful imperfections of craft.

He was always logical as well as humorous in his designing of forms and decorations related to function. He gives as examples *tisane* cups decorated with medicinal plants, a milk bowl of fresh appearance, its interior glazed '*d'un ton crémeux appétissant*'. Gallé's preference was for decorative motifs stylised from nature, and in his *notice* he explains that his references to nature are to be found in the very substance of his glazes and enamels as well as in the more obvious figurative decoration. With certain glazes, for example, he endeavoured to create an impression of the colour of the sky, cleansed by the rain, an idea which had been pursued by ancient Chinese ceramists. Other vases showed such a sky as a glimpse on the horizon, the body submerged by a sudden downpour

of water. A further example is of a country scene reserved on a ground of amber, symbolic and evocative of the warm, fleeting glow of twilight.

In some of his faience Gallé was inspired by quotations. A (misquoted) line from Shakespeare's *A Midsummer Night's Dream*, '*il faut qu'avant l'aube je suspende une perle à l'oreille de chaque primevère*', prompted Gallé to make a vase in the form of primrose corollas, the flowers splashed with droplets of silver-bearing enamel, sparkling like dew. Another vase, with rivulets of silver trickling through the glaze, bears and evokes the lines of Sully-Prudhomme[5]:

> *D'où viennent ces tremblantes gouttes?*
> *D'où viennent mes pleurs?*

The virtues of Gallé's faience lie more, however, in their wealth of invention than in their function as vehicles for poetic ideas. Roger-Marx admires the incredible wealth of ideas and techniques displayed in the ceramics,[5] and, after listing the range of objects created by Gallé's factory, vases and dishes of every shape and size, goblets, inkstands, lamp bases, clock cases, *torchères*, he dwells with particular fascination on the strange, comic, gothic bestiary which inhabits them, cats, cocks and hens, ducks, owls, swans in pairs, and parrots of azure blue richly ornamented in pale yellow.

For Gallé, his *oeuvre de terre* was merely the prelude to the more personal flights of fantasy which he was to develop further in his creations in glass and in wood. Even in his faience, however, one senses his growing awareness of the freedom of expression that could be achieved through technical mastery. An illustration of the artist's awareness can be found in his own words, delivered as a toast to the Chambre Syndicale de la Céramique et de la Verrerie, as he describes '... *La sensibilité, ... l'exaltation qui trouvent à l'usine scientifique moderne un terrain vierge pour s'envoler au pays d'azur*....'[6] (The sensitivity ... the exaltation which find in a modern scientific workshop a virgin ground from which to take off into the blue.)

Detail of decorated faience vase. (Sotheby & Co.)

Wood

Sellette aux feuilles de bananier, c. 1900.
(Private Collection, New York)

Carpenter at work in the Gallé factory,
1890s. (Private Collection)

Emile Gallé had lovingly carved the body of a glass vase and, though certainly pleased with the results of his work, felt that this creation required an unusual stand to show it off to greatest advantage. He decided that the effect could best be achieved by carving a base in some exotic wood from the South Sea Islands, a wood of exceptional tint. So it was that, for the first time, Gallé visited the shop of a dealer in precious woods. The visit was a revelation: *'Je crus découvrir les Indes et L'Amérique'*.[1] He was astonished to observe, for instance, the purple quality acquired by the billets of amaranth in the shafts of sunlight, or the streaks of pink and of violet that appeared in the scented wood shavings. This was in 1885, and, although Gallé's first reaction was merely a desire to form a collection of examples of the most precious woods, his curiosity was so strongly aroused that within a year he could boast a fully staffed and equipped cabinet-making factory and within four years was able to send off his first major furniture exhibit to the Paris Universal Exhibition of 1889.

Gallé had no apprenticeship in working in wood, and so he enlisted a number of old local cabinet makers whom he could trust to execute his ideas, and from whom he could learn. In addition to these collaborators Gallé acknowledged his debt to Victor Prouvé and to Louis Hestaux for their help in creating graphic designs to be applied to furniture, for, let there be no doubt about it, Emile Gallé had relatively little talent as a draughtsman and needed their professional assistance.

Gallé's woodworking factory is described as incorporating a main building of two floors, a mechanical sawmill housing band saws and other equipment, a central lodge three storeys high, steam sheds and outbuildings, cellars for the storing of fine veneers and cabinet woods and sheds for the housing of more conventional woods to be used for structural elements. These buildings included offices, showrooms, a packing room and caretaker's quarters in addition to the various workshops for carpenters, cabinet makers and specialised craftsmen involved in sculpting, in making up marquetry designs, in colouring or in polishing. And, there was, of course, the wealth of reference to be expected from as thorough an organiser as Gallé, not only a library, but specialised study collections of natural history specimens. In the grounds spread the neat rows of decorative plants, grouped according to species, that served as living models for structural and two dimensional designs. The workshops were all very well lit, with both water and gas supplies laid on. Each workshop was heated by a central system with a slow combustion stove.

When possible, and on condition that it entailed no loss in quality, Gallé was happy to use motor driven tools. In creating the limbs or other structural parts of a piece of furniture, a pre-shaped blade, fitted into a plane, was used to carve the basic shape which would then be finished and detailed by hand. In the

interests of economy such a blade was fitted to a machine, nicknamed '*la toupie*', the spinning top, capable of building up a speed of three thousand revolutions per minute. After the finishing touches at the hands of a sculptor, the results were complex, decorative, yet inexpensive mouldings. The venture into cabinet-making involved handling subsidiary materials such as the bronze or iron required to adorn pieces of furniture as handles, lockplates, keys, hinges or decorative details, and the marble which topped certain early pieces. Gallé learned to work these metals, casting, patinating bronze, modelling and colouring iron. He speaks in 1900 of lockplates, chased, inlaid, then tinged a purplish blue by the use of a flame.[2] A distinct impression of discipline emerges, both in Gallé's own application to the study of new skills and, in a more general way, in his management of the factory. The layout of the workshops was carefully considered for maximum efficiency and for ease of supervision. Gallé even introduced a system of clocking as a double check. Workers on private commissions were issued with white cards, whilst those involved in normal output had coloured cards. The cards provided day by day details of work in hand, and when collected at the end of each day by the office staff indicated not only how many hours had been worked by each man, but also how many hours' labour should be added to the open accounts of each piece of furniture.

The stock taking and re-ordering of the woods was a job which involved special attention, for, with a permanent stock of several hundred woods, care was needed for each wood to be easily located and for its source to be known. In 1889 Gallé noted from his stock books that he had no fewer than six hundred woods available for use as veneers, providing an almost infinite variety of textures, of grains and of colours.[3] A tight system of numbering allowed quick access to the available woods. The designers who drew up the working plans for mar-

Bronze lockplate from a display case, *c.* 1900. (Musée de l'Ecole de Nancy)

quetry chose the woods from a numbered sample set of veneers and it was one man's full-time job to ensure that the numbered set corresponded with stocks held and to replenish these stocks when supplies ran low. The management kept a filed index so that when a number was quoted, both name and source of the wood could immediately be ascertained.

During the course of fifteen years of working in wood, Gallé evolved certain views, strong personal philosophies and theories on the subject of furniture design. These he set down in a lengthy article *Le Mobilier Contemporain orné d'après la Nature*, published in the *Revue des Arts Décoratifs* in November/December 1900. The essay emphasises Gallé's clear conviction in his own course, and his wit and perception as a commentator on the vagaries of his contemporaries, advocates of the 'Modern Style'. Gallé's first proposals concern the essential concepts of modernity and of beauty. To him modernity, far from involving stylistic novelty and self assertiveness, is quite simply the tailoring of furniture to suit the present needs. Modern furniture is that made by our own generation to our own taste, for our pleasure and adapted to the needs of daily life. As for beauty, it is to be found only in the pursuit of truth. '*Le nom de beauté au sens de vérité, et jamais.... l'acceptation fausse ou médiocre de joliesse sans caractère ou d'opulence dénuée d'esprit*'.[4] (Beauty meaning truth and never... the false acceptance of prettiness without character or opulence without thought.) The association of the ideals of truth and beauty has a certain ring of inevitability. Gallé succeeds, however, in adding to its significance as he elaborates: beauty is to be found only in the sympathetic application of the principles of natural growth, of the structure and linearity of nature, infinitely variable, infinitely exploitable. By faithfully following the natural lines of appropriately chosen plants one will synthesise the logic and essence of life itself and the

Above
Etagère aux ombellifères, 1900. (Contemporary photograph)

Two vitrines *aux ombellifères*, 1890s.
(Collection Félix Marcilhac, Paris; Private
Collection, New York)

Grand meuble d'appui, 1889. (Messrs. Christie, Manson & Woods)

results will, naturally and inevitably, be beautiful. Such contemporary furniture will reflect life, valuing the truth of nature above all artificial eclecticism. It will have character, for its lines are those of living, reacting organisms, and it will have feeling because the artist inspired by nature could not fail to express in his work the deep communion of his creative spirit with creation itself.

Logic, practicality, artistic sensitivity, human vitality and essential honesty —here are the qualities which Gallé endeavoured to distil into his work in wood. His particular creed of naturalism, by its dependence on the infinite yet permanent qualities of life, avoids the ephemeral pitfalls of styles constructed through artifice. He has a contemptuous disregard for 'style', commenting that to have or not to have style does not seem to be as tragic an alternative as that facing Hamlet. And he finds the plight of a generation that feels it has lost its style as absurd as the plight of Peter Schlemyl, who thought he had lost his shadow. The real tragedy would be a lack, not of style, but of character.

Seeing himself as a stable and rational force amongst the illogical exaggerations of his contemporaries, Gallé opposed false appearances or indulgence in extremes. Modern critics highlight him as one of the leading figures of the French Art Nouveau movement, yet he saw himself as quite outside the tenets of the 'Modern Style'. Mocking its extremes, he wrote of '.... *les pseudo-varechs et les vermicelles affolés dont on a pensé faire, avec beaucoup de talent, à l'occasion de 1900, un berceau où abriter le vingtième siècle....*'[5] (The pseudo-seaweed and crazed vermicelli that, albeit executed with great talent, were thought to make a suitable cradle for the birth of the twentieth century in 1900.) If this is what is meant by modern furniture, then Gallé would willingly don once again his powdered wig. It is all too easy for designers to lose sight

Grand meuble d'appui, detail of marquetry, 1889. (Messrs. Christie, Manson & Woods)

Vitrine aux Libellules, details of lockplate, 1904. (Collection Mr. and Mrs. Robert Walker)

Le Chêne, 1889. (Contemporary photograph)

Workbox, fruitwood marquetry, 1890s. (Musée de l'Ecole de Nancy)

of the ideal of appropriateness, of fitness for purpose. He emphasises that a piece of furniture must be made for use. It is all too tempting for them to imagine that the function of a piece of furniture is to attract the gaze of visitors to such international agglomerations of phenomena as that organised by M. Alfred Picard—the Paris Universal Exhibition of 1900.

After this initial statement of faith, Gallé gives advice of a more practical nature. He emphasises once again the importance of fitness for purpose. A designer should always select, in the concept of any piece, a theme suggested by its purpose. As an example, Gallé asks whether in the design of a cigar cabinet one should look for inspiration to architectural models like the Parthenon, Reims and Versailles. On the contrary, a far richer and more appropriate source of inspiration could be found in the stem, the flower and the leaf of the tobacco plant itself.

Gallé's dining table of 1892, *La Table aux Herbes Potagères,* made for M. Henri Vasnier of the house of Pomméry in Reims, offers us another good example of the close relation of decorative theme and function. In an open letter to Lucien Falize, published in the *Revue des Arts Décoratifs,*[6] Gallé clarifies his intentions: *'il est inutile de vous dire que la forme très simple du meuble fut soumise à sa destination et que celle-ci encore suggéra le thème décoratif, les herbes potagères.'* (There is no need to tell you that the very simple shape of this piece of furniture was dictated by its purpose and that this also suggested the decorative theme of pot herbs.) He then lovingly des-

Table aux quatres libellules, 1900. (Musée de l'Ecole de Nancy)

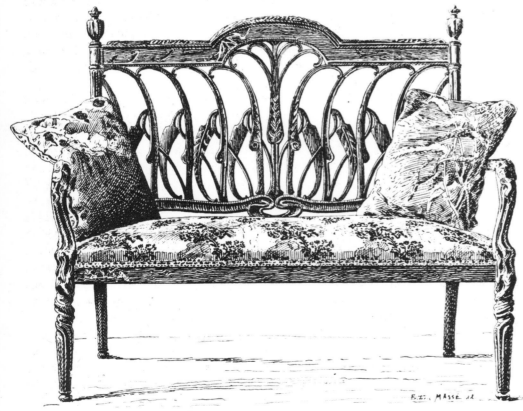

Wheatsheaf canapé, exhibited at the Universal Exhibition, Paris, 1900. (Contemporary engraving)

Commode à l'Ipoméa, 1900. (Bethnal Green Museum)

cribes the virtues of cabbage, parsley and of cucumber and explains how these humble occupants of the kitchen garden take on a special beauty in the context of a piece of furniture, a dining table where their presence is so amply justified. Typical of Gallé's attention to detail is the presence, as part of the decoration, of the gold beetles and ichneumon flies that are frequent visitors to such gardens.

It would be a fallacy, however, to assume that Gallé invariably followed his own golden rule which he lays down in *Le Mobilier Contemporain.* His rich imagination and lively sense of fantasy encouraged him to conceive pieces of furniture that were merely vehicles for the exploitation of personal themes; function, in such cases, became entirely secondary to emotive power on an intimate and artistic level. More complex factors than those allowed for in his theoretical writings often dictated Gallé's choice of themes. On other levels, however, he showed himself a more faithful disciple of his own theories. This is the case when he divides the decoration of furniture into three categories and discusses each in turn. He distinguishes between the structural elements, framework, legs, supports, stretchers; superficial, sculpted detail-work; and, lastly, flat surfaces. Structural elements should be suggested by plant stems, both in their silhouette and their section. Gallé points out the uncanny resemblance between certain reeded stems and furniture mouldings in their harmonious patterns of shadow and highlight, of depth and relief. He remarks how astonishing it is that man has made so little use of nature's infinite repertory and gives the example of the limitless applications in oriental art of the bamboo alone. If one should ever tire of plant forms, fauna can be used as the model and the insect world can become a new encyclopaedia of forms.

Firescreen, 1900. (Bethnal Green Museum)

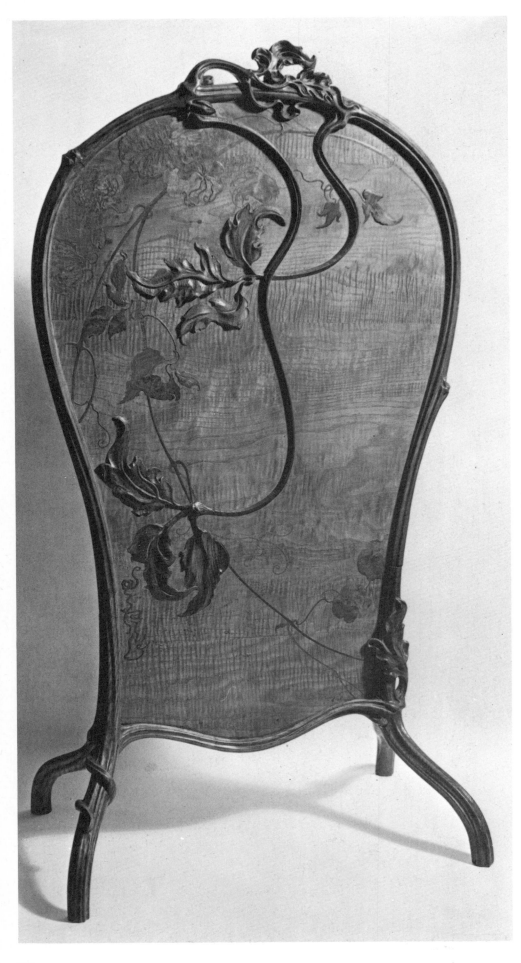

Detail of firescreen.

Gallé discusses the particular satisfaction he has found in the application of certain plant forms. The *umbellifer Heraclaeum Mantegazzium*, popularly called cow-parsley, first used by him in furniture design in 1894, became a particular favourite, and, certainly, this plant lent itself readily to elegant abstractions. Cow-parsley inspired cabinets, vitrines, tables, chairs, even bedroom suites. One critic, commenting on the *chaise aux ombelles* of 1902, finds an element of Japanese inspiration in this design, drawing a parallel between the form of the chair back and certain Japanese *tsuba* or sword-guards.[7] Others see cow-parsley as a symbol of local pride, for the plant grew in abundance around Nancy. One may, however, uncover less obvious and more morbid an explanation for the powerful attraction it held for Gallé. Another plant of the same family *'la grande Cigüe'*, *Conium maculatum*, is the source

81

Left
Vitrine aux Libellules, 1904. (Collection Mr.
and Mrs. Robert Walker)

Detail of *Vitrine aux libellules.*

Cabinet, *c.* 1900. (Photo courtesy Maître Georges Blache)

Table aux fougères, c. 1900. (Private Collection, New York)

of the poison that filled Socrates' deadly cup, hemlock.

Whatever his motives, he wrote in his essay that a theme must be chosen and, following its linear inspiration, a logical structure established. Never should the application of detail crowd this basic structure; joints should be neither disguised nor concealed, but modelled naturalistically, after a study of the ways in which plant stems divide, leaves join their branch or flowers burst from their stalk. Gallé criticises the tendency of designers both of the Louis XV period and of the 'Modern Style' to over-indulge sculpted and applied decoration to the point where the essential structure of a piece is lost beneath swirling arabesques. A piece of furniture is above all a construction of wood, parts and panels; there is no virtue in endowing it with the fluid quality of cast or soft-modelled materials, bronze, papier-mâché or clay.

The final area of discussion is the treatment of flat surfaces. In the closing lines of his essay Gallé suggests to his readers a sequel for the following year to discuss the decoration of flat surfaces and the design of bronze or other metal details. The sequel never appeared. Clearly, though, his policy was to treat flat surfaces as fresh canvases on which to elaborate floral themes in the subtle juxtaposition of rich woods, to compose a graphic hymn to the glory of Nature and to her mysteries. Gallé was spontaneously sympathetic to the techniques of marquetry, and used them in novel and inventive ways. A commentator of 1898 attributes the late nineteenth-century revival of the *charmant procédé* of inlaying designs in wood entirely to him and to his protégé Louis Majorelle.[8] An innovation peculiar to Gallé was the use of inlays carved in relief, standing out from their background. It can be found in his first exhibit of furniture in such pieces as the *Grand Meuble d'Appui* of 1889 which incorp-

Vitrine au blé, c. 1900. (Collection Mr. and Mrs. Sydney Lewis)

Fruitwood marquetry tray on the theme of the vine, *c.* 1900. (Private Collection)

orated orchids and bizarre insects in relief from the panels. A ladybird carved in red wood rests on a leaf with furled edges, whilst on the drawer below an orchid, its petals undulating in slight relief, bares a set of pale wood teeth and sticks out a lascivious tongue through lurid red wood lips, the horrific effect heightened by the sculpting of the details. Insects of other materials added to the richness and variety: a ladybird carved in red glass rests, like a cabochon jewel, on a wood leaf, butterflies spread wings that shimmer with the inclusion of mother-of-pearl. The '*lit papillon' Aube et Crépuscule* is a tour de force of marquetry with its relief carving and spangled sequin-like mosaics of mother-of-pearl. The elegant tendrils of the Donaldson Bequest firescreen of 1900 are another sophisticated example of Gallé's individuality in marquetry.

Gallé's first exhibit of furniture was the substantial group of pieces sent to the Exposition Universelle of 1889. Here he designed the wood structures to house certain of his creations, a cloison in amaranth and bog oak, a polygonal pavilion eight metres high with central glass display cabinets and a glass cupola. Most impressive was the *Grand Vestibule*, an arguably grotesque kiosk fifteen metres high, its decoration dedicated to the fossils of vegetation, in carved beechwood and blue-grey ash.

Gallé itemised his major exhibits in his *Notice sur la production de Menuiserie et Ebénisterie sculptées et marquetées d'Emile Gallé, 11 juin 1889*. Technically fascinating, sometimes guilty of stylistic eclecticism, they should not, however, as first efforts, be subjected to excessive criticism. Gallé describes the cabinet, *Le Chêne*, built in two tones of bog oak, the structure and details derived from the oak, and with four figurative panels, sculpted after designs by Victor Prouvé, inspired by the *Poèmes Antiques* of Leconte de Lisle; and the *Grand Meuble d'Appui*, constructed in ebony from Madagascar and acacia cut across the section, decorated with orchids and exotic insects. Conventional in its form, this piece displays exceptional invention in the details and shows the

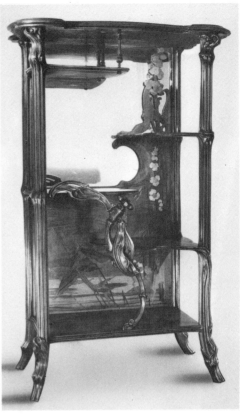

Etagère aux libellules, c. 1900. (Courtesy Maria de Beyrie)

Detail of *Etagère aux libellules.*

influence of Japanese *kumai* marquetry in the overlapping scale patterns created by the fan-shaped sections of red acacia. Purchased in 1892 by an Englishman, it was shipped back to France at Gallé's request for the Paris Universal Exhibition of 1900.[9] From 1889 also date the rather ponderous table *Je Tiens au Coeur de France* and a variety of other pieces, including tea and games tables, commodes and a *Grande Table pour Salon de Campagne.*

The first powerful manifestation of Gallé's naturalism appeared in the dining room created for Monsieur Vasnier of Reims and exhibited at the Salon du Champ de Mars in 1892 and 1893. The dining table *aux Herbes Potagères* has been mentioned already. The suite also included chairs, a massive sideboard, *Les Chemins d'Automne,* and a *console-desserte, Du Soir au Vignoble.* Gallé wrote a lengthy letter to Monsieur Vesnier as the craftsman put the finishing touches to the sideboard and its creator prepared to bid it farewell. The letter describes how the work was inspired by its own joy in being magnificent, dense and luxuriant; it was a song of praise to the warmth and abundance of harvest, a credo, expressed in the accents of autumn, a representation of might, growth and majesty, whose festal gleam and orchestral shimmer

Chair *aux ombellifères, c.* 1900. (Musée de
l'Ecole de Nancy)

would reflect not only the fanfares of life but also its muted voices and theo-
logical graces.[10] Deeply impressed by this work, Roger-Marx recalls the sideboard rising up from the floor as if from a fertile patch of earth.[11] 1893 was
also the year of the poignant table *Flore de Lorraine, Gardez les Coeurs
qu'avez Gagnés.*

At the Salon du Champ de Mars of the following year, Gallé exhibited his
two major religious pieces—the *Tabernacle du Saint Graal* and the cabinet
Les Fruits de L'Esprit. The same Salon was to be the venue, in 1895, of Gallé's
grande commode, Les Parfums d'Autrefois, its '*...faces mosaïquées de tout
le jardin des anciens baumes*'.[12] 1896 saw the creation of a small but important
piece, the cabinet *Les Fleurs du Mal*, inspired by Baudelaire's anthology of
'*fleurs maladives*'.[13] Gallé exhibited little during the next few years, holding
back designs for the 1900 Universal Exhibition. A most exciting spectacle
awaited those privileged to receive from Gallé a catalogue and invitation to the
opening in one of the envelopes specially printed in pastel, *japonisant* shades.
His style had matured. A sense of lightness and of elegance replaced the ponder-
ousness typical of too many of his earlier creations. Here were furnishings and

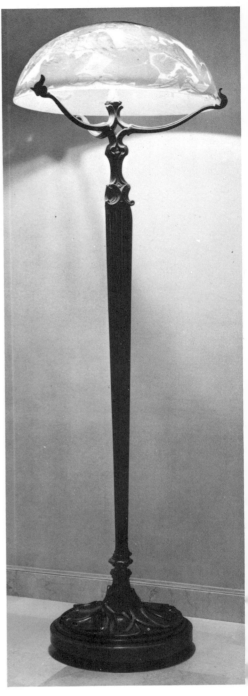

Standard lamp in wood, glass and bronze and two details, *c.* 1900. (Collection Mr. and Mrs. Robert Walker)

'...surroundings that suggest kings and courtiers'.[14] The elegant openwork *canapé*, *fauteuil* and chair on the theme of wheat sheaves, the *Etagère aux Ombellules*, the desk *La Forêt Lorraine* and the celebrated *Table aux Trois Libellules* all featured in this Exhibition, as did various commodes, including *Les Tulipes Turques* in Turkish walnut, and the *Commode à L'Ipoméa*, now part of the Donaldson Bequest, the worktable, carved in ash and walnut and inlaid with the legend '*Travail est Joie chez Gallé,*' and the firescreen carved in ash, decorated with oak, zebra-wood and sabicu, amboyna and walnut, also part of the Donaldson Bequest, the ungainly cabinet *La Montagne*, and the too-slavishly naturalistic buffet *Le Renouveau*. Gallé once again designed wood vitrines and display areas, among which his *Vitrine des Granges*, conceived on the lines of wheat stems and sheaves, was particularly successful. At the Salon of 1902, Gallé exhibited his *Corbeille de Noce*, which was according to de Fourcaud a delightful dowry chest, the framework modelled on virginia creeper and the panels showing glimpses of unknown shores and enigmatic inlets.[15]

It was in 1904 that the *magistrat* Henry Hirsch, on the occasion of his marriage, gave Gallé, in the last year of his life, his greatest commission, the massive, awesome *Vitrine aux Libellules*, carved in sombre and melancholy ironwood and bog oak, and the sumptuous bed *Aube et Crépuscule*. Extending the allusion, made by René d'Avril, to the bed as Gallé's symbolic catafalque, it is tempting to see the dark surrealistic dragonflies supporting the vitrine, their bulging eyes blown in iridescent *clair-de-lune* glass, as Emile Gallé's mournful pall-bearers. With sad irony, these two creations at once celebrate a marriage and herald a death. They were the last great pieces to distil the magic of Gallé's deep involvement, the last pieces '...*par lui dessinées, exécutées sous ses yeux, d'après ses pensées, avec son incessant secours.*'[16] (...designed by him, executed in his presence, according to his thoughts, with his constant help.)

Glass

One evening Monsieur Louis de Fourcaud had the good fortune to be admitted into the nerve centre of Gallé's operations—the spartan atelier, furnished only with shelves, a table and a chair where he dreamed up new ideas and where partly-finished vases awaited the master's finishing touches.[1] The table was littered with plant specimens, sketches and sheets of paper filled with the black ink of Gallé's cramped scrawls. These could be chemical formulae, quotations from the Bible or lines of poetry dear to Gallé, read and re-read until every shade of meaning had been absorbed and interpreted. '*Habite la terre et t'y nourris de vérité*'; the plea of Marceline Desbordes-Valmore—'*Béni soit le coin sombre où s'isole mon coeur*', and Maeterlinck's cry of hope—'*une belle chose ne meurt pas sans purifier quelque chose*' were amongst the lines which remained vivid in de Fourcaud's memory. It was in this room that Victor Prouvé depicted Gallé—long, sensitive, milky-white hands emerging from broad, starched cuffs, a proud brow, unruly hair brushed back, intense gaze, totally involved in his work, surrounded by vases filled with plant specimens which were for him, as they were for Baudelaire's *voyageurs solitaires*, the umbilical cord linking him to nature. *La Garenne*, the family home, was only a few hundred yards away, but for Gallé, in the act of creation, nothing had meaning or existence except the ideas which filled his mind and drove him on.

Prouvé's portrait shows us the very plainest furniture and dull, grey walls, yet the room was as rich as a palace, and de Fourcaud was totally captivated by the effects of colour and texture as the shafts of evening light played on the surfaces of the thirty or so vases in the room. '*Une coupe jaune, ensanglantée de rouges marbrures, frappée à revers d'un rayon qui la traversait, brillait d'une intérieure lueur de veilleuse gardienne d'un mystère . . . Un comet blanc comme nacre se nuait de rose chair, de mauvre et de vert pâle . . . Cà et là, l'améthyste, l'opale, la topaze brulée, le saphir clair, souriaient dans leur douceur blonde, à l'éclair saignant d'un rubis, au vert-scintillement d'une émeraude. L'émail onctueux s'était coulé, parfois, au creux des gravures, et, parfois, il déployait à la surface de chatoyantes broderies*'. (A yellow cup, bloodied with red streaks, struck on the surface by a ray of light, shone with the inner glow of a nightlight watching over some mystery . . . A pearly-white clouded with flesh-pink, mauve and pale green . . . Here and there amethysts, opals, burnt topaze, clear sapphire smiled in their soft pallor at the blood-red flash of a ruby, the sparkling green of an emerald. Sometimes the unctuous enamel had sunk to the bottom of the engraving, at other times it unfurled some shimmering embroidery on the surface.)

The effects of colour and texture which so entranced de Fourcaud were the results of many years of relentless work. Having mastered the essential techniques of glassmaking, Gallé evolved an entirely personal quality, a harmonious

Enamelled glass vase after a Mamluk mosque lamp, *c.* 1880. (Sotheby & Co.)

Portrait of Emile Gallé by Victor Prouvé 1892. (Musée de l'Ecole de Nancy)

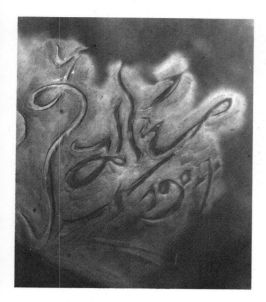

Detail of dragonfly bowl.

Carved and applied glass dragonfly bowl, 1904. (Private Collection, London)

Dragonfly bowl, marbled glass, carved and applied with a glass dragonfly in relief, in original suede presentation box, dated 1904. (Private Collection, London)

communion of technical and spiritual creative power. The turning point was the artist's appreciation of the possibility of treating glass as a semi-precious stone, making colour, texture and decorative effects integral parts of the glass body. His first phase, sometimes described as his transparent phase, lasted till about 1884. At the Exhibition of that year it became clear that Gallé was throwing off the shackles of other styles, making a break with eclecticism and asserting his own ideas.

During the 1870s, Gallé's glass could be said to fall into three broad categories—enamelled designs inspired from historical sources, enamelled designs of an already more personal quality, decorated with floral or insect motifs, and a third category involving more experimental methods of decoration. A great source of inspiration during this period were the enamelled glass creations of the Mamluk dynasty of Egypt and Syria (1250-1517 A.D.).[2] Gallé writes of the difficulties of these hard enamels, coloured in the mass in the manner of the Arabs and, subsequently, the Venetians. The problem is in making up an enamel that combines strength and resistance to atmosphere or acid, and which is of a chemical structure that will fuse satisfactorily to the body, yet without melting into it. When, around 1873, Gallé first experimented with hard enamels, he mastered only red, turquoise, white, opaque green, clear blue and gold. By 1884, however, he had added a large range of colours to his palette. The new shades included various reds and blues, blacks, yellows and greens, purples, pinks and violets, faded tones, powder blue, dull black and peach, and, most pleasing of all, subtle half-shades, greys and the colours of café-au-lait, of flesh and of ivory. He succeeded also in evolving translucent enamels to exploit the qualities of reflected and refracted light, and an enamel that was both translucent and colourless, to be applied like teardrops or splashes of rain.

Gallé's stylistic borrowings were haphazard and certain pieces incorporate

Enamelled blown glass gourd, 1880s. (Sotheby & Co.)

Right
Etched and carved cameo glass vase, in Egyptian taste, with glass cabochon and scarab decoration, 1890s. (Collection Alain Lesieutre)

Béni soit le coin sombre . . . , cased glass vase, 1890s. (Sotheby & Co.)

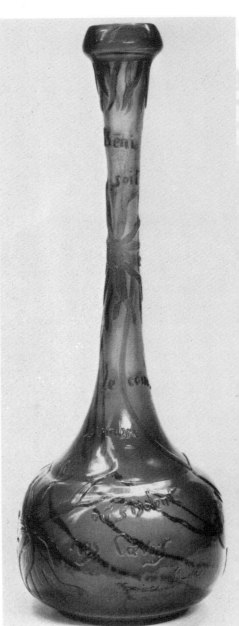

motifs taken from carpet and textile, pottery or metalwork designs, as well as from glass. A recent critic has pointed out the source of an enamelled casket of 1878 in the Musée de L'Ecole de Nancy as a Sicalo-Arabic ivory model of the thirteenth century.[3] Gallé was not always strictly correct in his re-creation of ancient models—thus his copies of enamelled mosque lamps are applied with figurative decorations which, by Muslim law, would have been forbidden in any mosque.

Other decorative themes were drawn from European mediaeval legend—glorious knights and their ladies were reserved on elaborate pseudo-heraldic grounds. A series of vases, drinking glasses, and decanters, at least one of which featured in the 1884 Exhibition, were enamelled with characters from François Villon's *Ballade des Dames du Temps Jadis*. Renaissance rock crystal *tazze* and Silesian eighteenth-century sweetmeat glasses inspired stemmed dishes, mould blown and enamelled, and, indeed, this form was never forgotten. The *coupe*, *La Violette*, of 1900, though the bowl itself is naturalistically modelled in full relief as the open flower, cannot escape comparison with this historical source. Ancient Egypt also suggested decorative ideas. A chunky clear glass vase, finely engraved and enamelled with a grasshopper in flight over splashed green chemical inclusions, is further decorated with an engraved and gilt frieze-like drawing of Egyptian harvesters. This piece, described as a *porte-cigares* was included in the 1884 Exhibition.

The 1884 Exhibition featured a substantial selection of glassware coloured in the mass, and with inclusions of metal foil: the blues, purples, yellows, reds, greens, and blacks now possible were the fruit of experiments with the oxides

Cased glass vase, blue on white, of Chinese inspiration, 1890s. (Collection Victor Arwas)

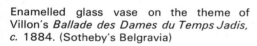

Enamelled glass vase on the theme of Villon's *Ballade des Dames du Temps Jadis, c.* 1884. (Sotheby's Belgravia)

Carved glass seal, 1890s. (Collection Alain Lesieutre)

Enamelled bowl with *'hyalite'* decoration, dedicated to Georges Flach, 1888. (Collection John Scott)

Enamelled gilt *clair-de-lune* glass vase, after 1878. (Sotheby & Co.)

of iron, cobalt, manganese, copper and chromium. Effects could not be fully controlled, however, by the glassmaker, and such glass, coloured in the mass, was still only possible for the luxury and not the commercial market. No two vases were alike, and the decorator was obliged to invent decorative schemes according to the chemical accidents. A *coupe*, haphazardly marbled in black glass, included three areas of opaque black cleverly developed by Louis Hestaux as Night, Silence, and Darkness; another vase, the colours of flawed amethyst with inclusions of air bubbles, was decorated with a woman and cherubs blowing soap bubbles, the flaws turned to decorative effect. Gallé's decription of the colour of this vase as resembling flawed amethyst was no accident; he was proud to display vases resembling this and other stones, agates, jades or quartz. His first notable venture in colouring glass in the mass had been his *clair-de-lune* glass which achieved great popularity when first exhibited in 1878. A small inclusion of cobalt oxide gave it an opalescent tint which turned a sapphire blue in certain lights. The Musée des Arts Décoratifs was interested enough to purchase a sample in 1878 and rival manufacturers imitated the effect, known as *Mondschein* in Germany and 'Moonlight' glass in England. Elaborations of the technique were exhibited by Gallé in 1884.

New skills were on show in 1884 – refinements of the engraver's art, combinations of engraved enamel, enamel set in areas cut away by the engraver, engraved cabochons, all the work executed by hand with an engraver's wheel. Gallé disclaimed the use of hydrofluoric acid which could, he said, be of absolutely no use in achieving the artistic effects he was pursuing. Possibly the most notable innovations of 1884 were Gallé's declarations in his *Notice sur la Production du Verre* that the most satisfactory decorative motifs were those drawn from local flora and fauna, that forms should relate to function, and that he now welcomed '*L'intervention féconde du sentiment dans le décor du verre.*'

The achievements of 1884, however, are dismissed by Gallé[4] as naive in comparison with his exhibits sent to the Paris Exhibition of 1889. The three hundred pieces which, in section 19 of the Exhibition, encompass his new skills, include new colourings, new internal effects, more sophisticated imitations of stones, new enamels and enamelling techniques. They also show a greater freedom in the interpretation of nature, as well as the influence of Chinese and Japanese art.

Gallé describes yellows and lustrous brown and greenish tones derived from silver and sulphur, a peacock-blue from copper and altogether new and precious colours from iridium and thallium. By 1889 he had command of no fewer than one hundred distinct colours which could be combined in countless permutations. He devotes a paragraph to a new black glass, '*hyalite*', the sad and sombre tones of which are relieved by underlays of other colours, and by a grey sheen in the black which Gallé attributes to a partial reduction in the carbon-laden furnace fumes of the component iron peroxide. This glass was used in a series of morbid *vases de tristesse*, made to celebrate sadness or death. A carved '*hyalite*' *vase de tristesse* in the Musée des Arts Décoratifs is a respectful tribute '*A des forêts qui ne sont plus*':[5] a small bowl, enamelled and with internal splashes of '*hyalite*' offers homage '*A Georges Flach de Strasbourg, Docteur en droit, Not. officer de l'armée française de réserve, mort à Nancy 1886. Son ami Emile Gallé. Dilexit Patriam Speravit Restitutam.*'[6] The most celebrated *vase de tristesse* is perhaps that acquired by the Musée des Arts Décoratifs at the 1889 Exhibition, which depicts Orpheus in the murky Stygian vapours of the underworld separated from a fainting Eurydice.

Amethyst, quartz, jade, agate, alabaster, onyx, amber or tortoiseshell, all could now be simulated with far greater control than was possible in 1884. Lustre effects, or *flambés*, could be achieved by the reducing or oxidising action of the furnace heat on the body of vases coated with appropriate chemicals. Streaks and splashes of colour could, with precision, be trapped between layers

Designs for flower-form vases, contemporary engraving after an original drawing by Gallé, before 1889.

Flower-form vase based on the arum lily, 1890s. (Private Collection, London)

Left
Vase Orphée, carved cameo glass *vase de tristesse,* 1889. (Musée des Arts Décoratifs)

of glass as could chemical reactions. Gallé had discovered chemicals capable of turning to gas within the warm glass and of creating a mass of minute bubbles, each lined with a lustrous deposit.

1889 saw the introduction of a wealth of new enamels, gold-based pinks, lilacs, oranges, new reds, violets and purples. New technical tours de force included single pieces decorated with a variety of enamels fired at different temperatures, *champlevé* enamels fired in intaglio and gilt settings and a selection of *émaux bijou,* tinted cabochons of enamel fired over metal foil in imitation of emeralds, rubies, topaz, or naturalistic effects such as the sheen of a scarab's back or the eyes of a dragonfly. Louis de Fourcaud reproduces a delightful drawing, executed before 1889, in which Gallé proposes forms for vases and *flacons* based on the elegant spirals of the arum lily. Their import-

Flower-form decanter set. (Sotheby & Co.)

ance lies in their essential form, and not merely their decoration, being derived from nature. The lines of the arum lily are adapted not simply to the decoration, but, more meaningfully, to the entire conception of these glass objects.

Finally, mention must be made of the Chinese and Japanese influence on the glass exhibited at Paris in 1889. A Japanese elegance, interpreted but not imitated, is undoubtedly present in the graphic representations of plant motifs, an elegance that was henceforth to characterise Gallé's work, with occasional more or less overt acknowledgement to Japanese art. Chinese forms were borrowed: a small green overlay glass phial modelled as a scarab, its head the stopper, resembles traditional Chinese cased glass snuff bottles, and certain vases echoed the contours of Chinese archaic bronze vessels. One of Gallé's new colours, a sealing-wax red, bore an uncanny resemblance to *tsuishu* lacquer. Gallé even introduced a new signature with an oriental flavour—the name Gallé incised in fine script, vertically, in elaborate almost undecipherable letters. The important innovation, however, was his new series of cameo vases, incised through two or more layers of coloured glass, and derived directly from Chinese cased glass vases of the Ch'ien Lung period.

Marqueterie sur verre was the name given by Gallé to his next major technical innovation, first perfected in 1897 and presented to the public at the Salon du Champ de Mars of 1898. *Marqueterie* involved the building up of the decoration of a piece by pressing lumps of coloured glass into the warm, soft body, rolling the surface on a marver to smooth the insets which, when cool, would be given identifiable form by wheel carving. The high risk of breakage involved in heating and re-heating vases to keep the glass soft and workable made this an expensive craft, most frequently reserved for special pieces,

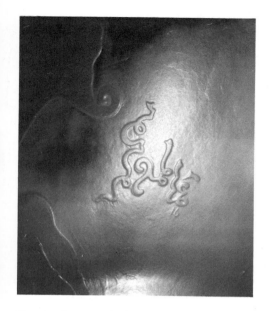

Cameo signature in Japanese taste, detail.

Etched and polished cameo glass vase, 1890s. (Sotheby & Co.)

either *pièces uniques* or those produced in very small editions. The popularity of certain designs, however, demanded their manufacture in series and *marqueterie sur verre* occupied the highest echelon on the scale of Gallé's commercial output.

1900, and the Paris Universal Exhibition. Gallé was able once again to surprise his public and disappoint his imitators with breathtaking feats of glassmaking; there were a few new skills but, above all, an unprecedented daring in combining techniques and treating the glass as a medium to be freely sculpted. By the effects of chemical reaction, or by the deliberate decomposition or gritting of the surface, the natural textures and sheens of either plants or animals were recreated in glass.

Great skill was required for the deft work of applying relief masses of coloured glass to the surface of a vase and modelling them while soft, through constant reheatings at the furnace. *L'Orchidée*, *Le Lys* and the *flacons*, vases, and bowls *Des Roses de France* are fine examples of this sculptural approach, inaugurated in 1900. These and other outstanding experiments such as *La Violette* of 1900, the Surrealist hand, dripping with seaweed, of about 1900-1901, or the dragonfly bowl of 1904 were made in very small, what might be called proof editions of perhaps three or four, each trying a slight variant of colour or form, unlike special commissions or commemorative pieces which were *pièces uniques*.

103

Signature on spiral glass bottle, detail.

Spiral, speckled, glass bottle, 1880s.
(Sotheby & Co.)

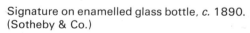

Signature on enamelled glass bottle, c. 1890.
(Sotheby & Co.)

Paper trade label, 1890s. (Collection N. Manoukian)

Paper trade label, 1890s. (Collection Alain Lesieutre)

Detail of base enamelled glass bowl, 1900. (Collection Amiel Brown)

Glass table lamp, c. 1900. (Contemporary photograph)

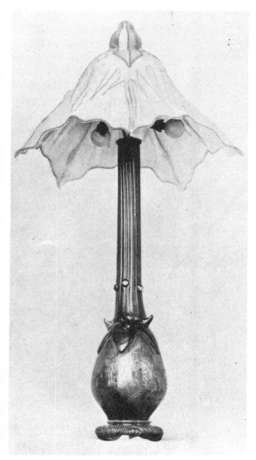

From the vantage point of 1900, Gallé looked back over his years of glass-making and, for the benefit of a curious public, created in the Exhibition a retrospective of every stage of his career. These pieces bear their original date of conception and the legend 'Reédité en sa Cristallerie pour l'histoire du Verre, 1900'.

During the last four years of his life, from 1900 to 1904, Gallé conjured with ideas for the decorative application of glass to electric lighting. Flower-form lamps concealed light fittings within half open petals, their fine veins thrown into relief by the light within. Glass flower-form shades, on stems of bronze or wrought iron, were designed for wall and for ceiling. The metal mounts for these lamps, as for many vases, were cast or wrought in Gallé's ateliers. The only known standard lamp combines a domed cameo shade with an elegant cast bronze and carved wood base and stem. Outstanding was the table-lamp Les Coprins of 1904, modelled as three giant mushrooms, destined for the Salon du Champ de Mars of 1905. Three versions of the lamp were made, over thirty inches high, blown and carved in glass of up to five layers with effects of metallic iridescence and fine silver leaf insertions, supported in wrought iron bases. Les Coprins surprises by the blatantly sensual admiration which it inspires; it has the disturbing effect of being very much out-of-scale, the discomfort of Surrealism. This one object, surely, above all others, is the épanouissement of Gallé's art.

Les Coprins is a work of art of great refinement and luxury. Such precious, adventurous creations, however, constituted a numerically small proportion of the atelier Gallé output and were subsidised and supported by the commercial production of decorative glassware. The duality of standards became expecially noticeable after 1889, when, in an apologia, Applications Industrielles, Vulgarisation Artistique,[7] Gallé justifies, with more or less good grace, the need to expand on a commercial basis. From this date began the production of ever-larger series of cased glass vases, the cameo effect achieved by the formerly disdained hydrofluoric acid, and substantial series of enamelled pieces. Research[8] has uncovered the facts that an industrial vase could cost as little as five francs, whereas hand-made pieces could cost anything from three hundred to about twelve hundred francs for the most elaborate pièces uniques. The differences in artistic merit are, probably, in roughly similar proportion.

The heart of Gallé's factory was his own atelier.[9] Close by and under his immediate supervision were the studios where his assistants designed silhouettes for the wooden or cast-iron glass-blowing moulds and prepared water-colour designs for enamellers, engravers and decorators to follow; in another studio, scientific minds researched formulae for new colours. The raw materials with their appropriate chemical admixtures were blended in drums and then carried in crucibles to be melted down. The bulk melting of the glass took

Detail of *L'Oignon* vase. This type of decoration was known as *martelé*.

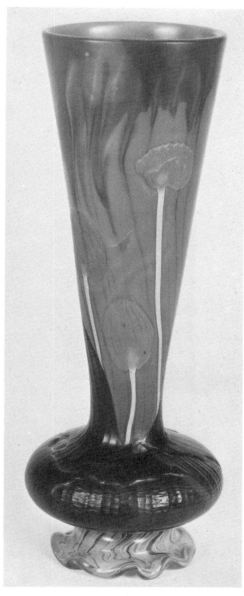

L'Oignon vase, deeply carved blown and overlaid glass with *marqueterie sur verre* decoration, dated 1900. (Collection Alain Lesieutre)

Top right and centre
Applying bitumen of Judea. (Contemporary photographs)

A view of a section of the Gallé factories. (Contemporary photograph)

Interior of glass-blowing workshops. (Private Collection)

Glass polisher. (Contemporary photograph)

place at a temperature of 1400-1450 C. in a Boëtius furnace with four melting pots, each with a capacity of 350 kilos of glass, heated by coal-gas burners. The molten glass was picked up by the blower on the end of his cane and then either free blown, shaped with the aid of tools, or blown into a hinged mould. In vases built up of several layers, these were fused together before final shaping. Elaborately wrought vases could spend weeks at the furnace, with long periods of cooling between each successive stage of creation. More conventional vases, cut from the blower's cane with large scissors, were taken to the annealing oven, to cool over a period of four days before being taken to the decorating studios. Too rapid a cooling of such thick glass would result in cracking.

Vases destined for enamelling were sent off to the appropriate workshops for the application of their decoration, which was then fired in muffle-furnaces. Special vases were sent directly to the engravers' workshops to be carved entirely by hand under the close supervision of one of the creative team. Commercial vases were covered in the white delineations of standard patterns and motifs and then sent to the workshops to be painted in positive in acid resistant bitumen of Judea. Heavy vases were worked on by men, lighter pieces by women or young girls, the sexes segregated in separate areas. These decorating workshops were large and airy, well lit with lofty windows and individual overhead lights; the work was done at tables that lined the walls, each worker had his stool, a shaped wood elbow rest perpendicular to the table on this right side, and his own brushes, rags and bowls of bitumen of Judea. Long centre tables held stocks of vases.

Glass decorators at work. (Private Collection)

From here the vases went to the acid baths—wood vats, lined in lead with powerful suction mechanisms above to remove the fumes of the 75% concentration of hydrofluoric acid. The dipping was effected by men wearing protective rubber gloves and old army surplus uniforms to protect their clothes from acid splashes. Then, back to the decorating rooms to be prepared for a second or third dip. The etching completed, a vase was then ready for the finishing touches, rough edges were polished off on large emery wheels, the ground of certain vases was given a final matting in a very weak solution of acid, or the surface was polished on cork wheels smeared with metallic putty. Other pieces had the benefit of a visit to the engraver's where more delicate tools added an interest to the mechanical finish of the acid; here were cutting wheels of all sizes including minuscule wheels for fine detail work, wheels of rose copper, brass, bronze, cork, wood or felt, coated with a mixture of emery powder, oil and turpentine. The engraver's work done, the vase was finished, apart from a final cleaning with soda, *potasse d'Amérique* or plain soap and water.

Le Chef des Odeurs Suaves

Henri Frantz wrote in March 1897, 'I am hardly exaggerating when I say that Monsieur Emile Gallé is at the moment, and by every right, the most conspicuous figure in the French world of art, for his is undoubtedly recognised as a master, and he alone in our day can now claim the honour of having formed a school, of having influenced a whole generation of younger artists, and given rise to a genuine revival of industrial art.'[1]

Gallé had become, in spite of himself, a public figure, the recipient of the *Legion d'Honneur* and important public and royal commissions. The table and glass for the Imperial Russian family, the *Vase Pasteur*, the *flacon* of rust-black and purple glass, *Je Vaincrai par Douceur*, offered by the association of distillers to the President of the Republic, all enhanced Gallé's public reputation. In 1884, he made a glass clock case, *La Fortune Endormie sur sa Roue*, intaglio engraved and enamelled in translucent violet and green and opaque ivory for Margaret, Queen of Italy. A delicate vase decorated with daisies and lilies, speckled with gold, was commissioned for the Princess Marguerite de Chartres, on the occasion of her marriage to the Duke of Magenta and shown at the Salon of 1897. Henri Frantz praised '. . . . the most curious and subtle impressions . . . .' in this '. . . . vase of virgin whiteness decorated with daisies and wreathed, as it were, with the lines of a poet in praise of the marguerite.'[2] Numerous exhibition pieces were bought directly by the State for the Musée des Arts Décoratifs or the Musée du Luxembourg.

Gallé won admiration from all sides, yet he remained an essentially introverted character, embarrassed by the sound of praise. He made no effort to cultivate purely social contacts amongst the aristocracy. On the contrary, de Fourcaud explains that, on the occasion of exhibitions in Paris, Gallé was on his way home to Nancy before the exhibition gates were even closed, leaving behind only the magic of his reputation.[3] On his rare visits to Paris, he always seemed very impatient to hurry home.

The impression given by de Fourcaud of his few meetings with Gallé is hardly that of encounters with a suave socialite—he describes him as 'thin, dry, extremely highly strung, with a tormented face, his speech uneven, sometimes slow, broken by silences, at other times speeded up as if impatient to transmit a rush of simultaneous ideas.'[4] A similar impression is given in the Goncourts' *Journal*. Gallé, *chez* Goncourt, is introduced to another guest who shares his interest in horticulture; they immediately strike up an intense conversation and their host records his amusement at 'Gallé's excitement, the mimicry of his scraggy body and his fevered eyes.'[5]

Certain aspects of Paris life held Gallé's interests, however—developments in the artistic world, new theatrical spectacles and the company of artists whose work he admired, of poets whose writings inspired him. He found satis-

Edmond de Goncourt photographed by Nadar. (Mansell Collection)

Cigar holder, enamelled, engraved, carved and gilt glass, exhibited Paris 1884. (Private Collection, London)

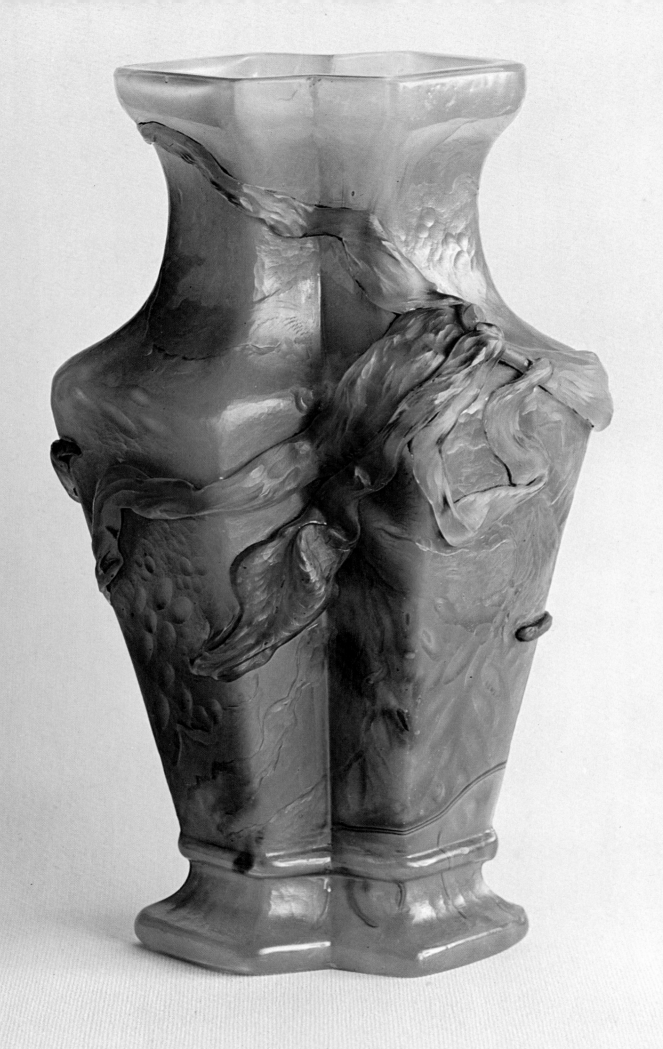

Emile Gallé in 1889. (Private Collection)

L'Orchidée, carved and applied glass vase, 1900. (Courtesy Maître Georges Blache)

faction in mixing with those elements of aristocratic society which associated closely with the artistic world, the sympathetic and creative patrons, the leaders of new fashions, the breeding ground of new ideas and interests, in short, those elements which perpetuated the ideals of aesthetic Paris *salon* society. The exchange of ideas that resulted from such associations undoubtedly enriched Gallé's mature work; this was particularly noticeable in the 1890s.

Perhaps it was at the suggestion of Paris friends, perhaps in their company that Gallé visited the Folies Bergère in 1893 for the spectacle of Loïe Fuller dancing in her first, sensational Paris season, at the beginning of a career that was to reach its ultimate triumphs seven years later at the 1900 Universal Exhibition. In October 1893 Gallé wrote with rapture of '. . . . *ces pourchas des jaunes et des rouges, ces métempsycoses de nuances dont se revêt cette magicienne aux reflets mouvants, la Loïe Fuller.*'[6] A photograph of Rupert Carabin's sculpture of Loïe Fuller, preserved amongst Gallé's personal effects, bears witness to his fascination with the dancer.[7] The English critic Charles Anet wrote in 1903 that 'Loïe Fuller has not merely served as a model for artists. She has been, by her creations, a source of inspiration to the applied arts, and

her influence is discernible in the revival of the decorative styles. The glass-working art owes her a great deal. Emile Gallé, the best master glassworker in France, freely admits that he was led to seek new colouring for his glass by seeing the beautiful light effects invented by Loïe Fuller.'[8] Such were the riches to be found in Paris.

Gallé was avid to absorb the cultural developments of his time and Roger-Marx certainly had a healthy respect for the richness of his friend's broad culture. '*Le long de la vie il tient commerce avec les esprits qui sont l'orgueil et la consolation de l'humanité; il vibre à l'unisson des poètes; il pénètre le secret des compositeurs héroiques; il se hause à l'examen des plus graves problèmes de la destinée. Tout ce qui touche à l'évolution de l'homme le passione, et l'on s'abuserait à l'imaginer prudemment confiné dans la sure retraite d'une tour d'ivoire. Il veut entendre les bruits du dehors et se mêler intimement à l'histoire de son temps.*'[9] (Throughout his life he maintained close relationships with men whose minds are the pride and solace of humanity. He vibrates in unison with poets, he penetrates the secrets of heroic composers

The Comtesse Greffulhe by Philip de Laszlo, 1902. (Courtesy Le Duc de Gramont)

—he encompasses the study of the gravest problems of human destiny. All that touches on the evolution of mankind fascinates him, and it would be entirely wrong to imagine him confined to the safe retreat of some ivory tower. He wants to hear the sounds of the outside world and mingle closely with the history of his time.)

The closely knit circle of aristocratic aesthetes that dominated artistic life in Paris towards the end of the nineteenth century warmly welcomed Gallé's talent; they showed sympathy for his work, appreciated his ideals and shared many of his interests. The Count Robert de Montesquiou, with whom Gallé shared long relations, surely helped open many doors including that, for example, of the Comtesse Greffulhe, née Elisabeth Caraman-Chimay, considered one of the most beautiful women in French society. This dark-haired beauty had the good sense to marry an immensely wealthy descendant of Louis XV who was prepared to remain in the wings while his wife held court for her artistic friends. The Comtesse, whose salon was amongst the most exclusive in Paris, was Count Robert's cousin, and it was surely he who introduced Gallé to her.

Marcel Proust. (Radio Times Hulton Picture Library)

Count Robert de Montesquiou by Helleu. (Photo courtesy Lady Abdy)

Japanese art was doubtless the subject of long conversations, for it was a passion shared by all three. The Comtesse would invite small groups of friends with mutual interests either to her villa in Dieppe or to her country home, Boisboudran, an ugly chateau enlivened by the efforts of a Japanese gardener. Count Robert was frequently at hand to stage-manage such aesthetic gatherings, at which the guests might include Antonio La Gandara, Paul-César Helleu or Jaques-Emile Blanche. Gallé made for the Comtesse, around 1890, a *coupe mystérieuse*, to match the fascination of the woman who was the inspiration for Marcel Proust's Duchesse de Guermantes.[10]

Another of Count Robert's introductions was, regrettably, the occasion of a rather unpleasant scene between the Count and a third guest. Montesquiou had prevailed upon his friend, the Baroness Adolphe de Rothschild, to graciously open her home to a small group of the Count's artist friends, so that they

Marbled glass vase with applications of *verre églomisé, c.* 1900. (Collection Alain Lesieutre)

might have the privilege of meeting her, and of viewing her art collection. Gallé was one of a group which included La Gandara and Sem (the cartoonist). The Baroness had, on her own initiative, invited the poet Henri de Régnier, his wife and two sisters-in-law, with whom Count Robert was not on the best of terms. The visit ended with a recital by Delafosse, the Count's pianist, and it was during this musical interlude that Gallé became the unwilling spectator of an argument that ended in a duel between the Count and the poet.

A story told by Marcel Proust bears witness to a more serious acquaintanceship, the deep attachment felt by Gallé for the Princess Bibesco. Proust gives the details in a long letter to her son Prince Antoine Bibesco, cousin of the beautiful and magnetic Princess Marthe Bibesco, whom Montesquiou tried so hard to manipulate. Proust had made the journey to see Gallé to discuss the details of a vase, only to be told by one of the employees that the factory

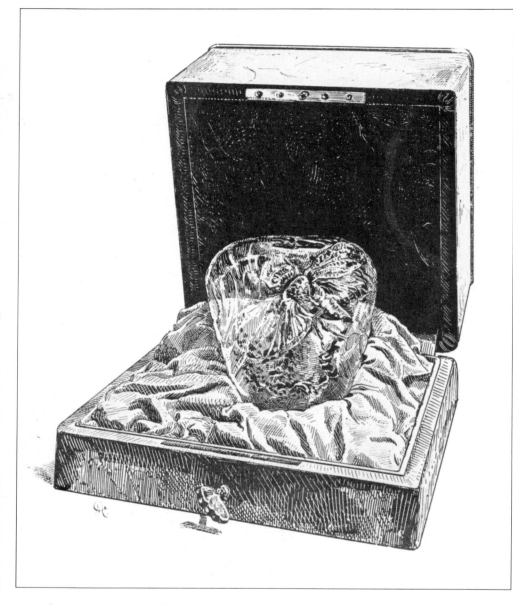

The Comtesse Anna de Noailles. (Radio Times Hulton Picture Library)

Le cri strident de mon désir, late 1890s. (Contemporary engraving)

was closed because Gallé *père* had died that very day 3 December 1902. Proust replied that Emile Gallé must be deeply grieved by this loss, but the employee retorted that Monsieur Gallé had not yet been informed of his father's death. Monsieur Gallé was already in such a state of grief and, as a result, in such poor health that no one dared break further bad news lest the shock prove fatal. Proust asked if Gallé's grief was due to his father's illness, but apparently even this had been kept secret from him. He was in a state of deep depression, he was seeing no one and all activity was forbidden him. The reason for his misery and debility was the death one month previously, of one of the people whom he admired most in this world, the Princess Bibesco.[11]

Marcel Proust was deeply touched by such a display of affection and respect on the part of a man whose work he so greatly admired. Proust had first been made aware of Gallé's genius by Count Robert de Montesquiou, and, for Proust, the name of Gallé was inseparable from the of the Count.[12] He proposes the Count as the finest of guides to Gallé's work either in person or through the pages of his masterly essay on Gallé contained in the volume of critical writings published in 1897, *Les Roseaux Pensants.* Proust was captivated by the subtle qualities of Gallé's work. In his correspondence he shows a curiosity about the glass, admiring the quality of the enamels and of the deep engraved work.[13] Elsewhere, it is the artist's sensitivity to wood which arouses

Glass flacon, etched cameo over gold foil inclusions, engraved *'graine de l'Orme Samain, Gallé 1900*. (Collection Félix Marcilhac, Paris)

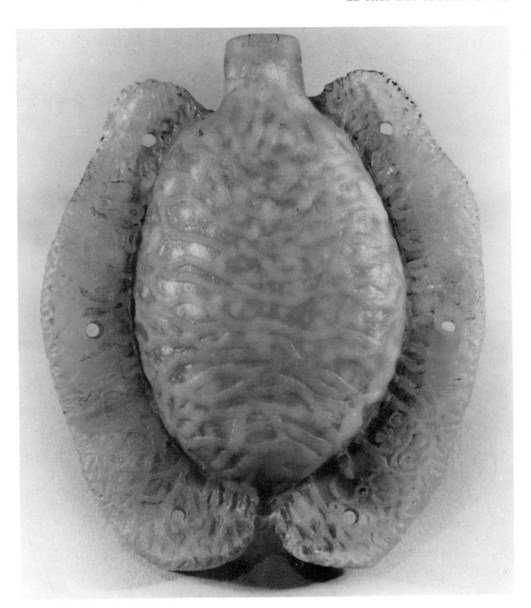

his admiration. He writes for instance of '. . . *ces nobles accents que Monsieur Gallé a su tirer du coeur harmonieux des chênes . . . ces admirables oppositions de tons. où la feuille se détache d'une autre couleur que la tige.*'[14] (. . . those noble strains which Monsieur Gallé has drawn from the harmonious hearts of oak trees . . . those admirable contrasting tints, the leaf standing out against the background of the stem.) Proust was particularly sensitive to the layers of mood and of mystery which enshrouded Gallé's creations, to the variety of subjective interpretations possible within each piece, and to their evocative strength. In turn, Proust captured moments in nature which brought to mind the colours and textures of the glass. *A La Recherche du Temps Perdu* describes two such moments, the first evoking Gallé's *verre églomisé*, glass with a suspension of white particles within a clear body, as symbol of winter snow—'*Bientôt l'hiver; au coin de la fenêtre, comme un verre de Gallé, une veine de neige durcie.*'[15] (Soon winter, and at the corner of the window pane, as on a piece of glass by Gallé, a hardened streak of snow.) And for a moment, it is the foaming of the sea that calls to mind certain vases—'*La mer . . . effilochait sur toute la profonde bordure rocheuse de la baie des triangles empennés d'une immobile écume linéamentée avec la délicatesse d'une plume ou d'un duvet dessinés par Pisanello, et fixés par cet émail blanc, inaltérable et crémeux qui figure une couche de neige dans les verreries de Gallé.*'[16] (The sea . . . unravelled on the deep rocky

EMILE GALLÉ

shore of the bay, triangles finned with a still foam, as soft as a feather or down drawn by Pisanello and set with that unchanging, creamy, white enamel which represents a layer of snow in Gallé's glass.)

Proust communicated his enthusiasm to his friends and pestered Gallé for vases, commissioning them as special gifts for close friends. The glassmaker was not always able to fulfil Proust's requests. Fernand Gregh, a friend for whom Proust commissioned a vase to celebrate his marriage, tells of the author's disappointment at Gallé's being unable to complete the piece in time for the wedding.[17] The Comtesse de Noailles records a vase given to her as a New Year present by the author.[18] Gallé, at Proust's request, had tried on several occasions to inscribe in glass the eight lines from *Eblouissements* in which her hands, compared to woodland springs and Japanese porcelain, preserve the secret tracings of the bodies of ferns. The effort was unsuccessful and the vase, decorated with intermingled ferns, was given to the Comtesse who described it as '. . . *muet, mais d'un goût ravissant.*' This was certainly not the only Gallé vase enjoyed by Anna de Noailles. The young woman, whose volumes of verse soon won her acclaim among artistic circles, was a friend and an inspiration to Gallé. A translucent vase, illustrated by de Fourcaud[19] in the luxury of its fitted presentation case, takes its theme from a verse by the young Comtesse—'*Le cri strident de mon désir . . .*' Another vase,[20] dedicated by Gallé to the Comtesse, reveals his depth of human feeling. In two shades of purple decorated with an iris in carved blue glass, it is an invocation to her to champion the cause of Dreyfus. The lines are by Maeterlinck. '*Toutes les âmes sont prêtes, il faut cependant que l'une d'elles commence. Pourquoi ne pas oser être celle qui commence . . . .*' Gallé had been amongst the first to champion the cause of Dreyfus, eagerly putting his name to the petition of January 1898. It is with a note of sadness that Madame Gallé refers to her husband's efforts, his letters and articles in the local and national press in the fight for justice.[21] A *bureau de dame*, made by Gallé for his wife, has survived as a memorial to the struggle. It is dedicated with the inscription '*A ma brave femme, Henriette Gallé, en mémoire des luttes patriotiques pour les principes d'humanité, de justice et de liberté. Mai 1899. Emile Gallé, trésorier de la ligue française pour la défense des Droits de l'Homme et du Citoyen.*' Roger-Marx also pays posthumous respect to Gallé's spontaneity and unselfishness in this cause.[22]

Marcel Proust and Anna de Noailles were but two of Gallé's contacts in the literary world. Another author and leader of fashion whose taste he respected was Edmond de Goncourt, who commissioned at least one work from Gallé, a goblet as a gift for Alphonse Daudet.[23] Details of the large dinner given in 1895 to celebrate de Goncourt's appearance in the honours lists give a suggestion of the company kept by Gallé, although on this occasion he was unable to be present. The guest list included the names of Frantz Jourdain, Raymond Poincaré, Ministre de l'Instruction Publique, Sully-Prudhomme, Marcel Prévost, Puvis de Chavannes, Alfred Stevens, Paul-César Helleu and Alphonse Daudet. There is, however, one name not mentioned by de Goncourt, which yet dominates the scene.

If the name of Count Robert de Montesquiou recurs with such regularity in the story of Gallé's contacts with the Paris artistic world, it is because the Count, with characteristic vanity, regarded Gallé as perhaps his greatest conquest, a conquest made through the intermediary of Montesquiou's anthology of verse *Les Chauves-Souris*, published in 1892. The volume made a strong impression on Gallé who created a number of works inspired either by specific lines or by the mood of the verse which it contained. Montesquiou was flattered that his writings '. . . *avaient inspiré des compositions . . . dans lesquelles les découpures du volatile bizarre se mêlent à celles des nuages, aux noms des constellations et à la tonalité des brumes.*'[24] (. . . had inspired compositions in which the indenta-

Glass hand, streaked and marbled blown glass with applied decoration, *c.* 1900. (Private Collection, Paris)

Page 122
Blown glass vases with applied decoration of *verre églomisé,* the one on the left engraved '*Gallé Dombasle-s-Meurthe Solvay et Cie 1873-1903.* (Collection N. Manoukian)

Page 123
Vase Libellule, iridescent glass with carved, applied decoration, dated 1900. (Collection N. Manoukian)

120

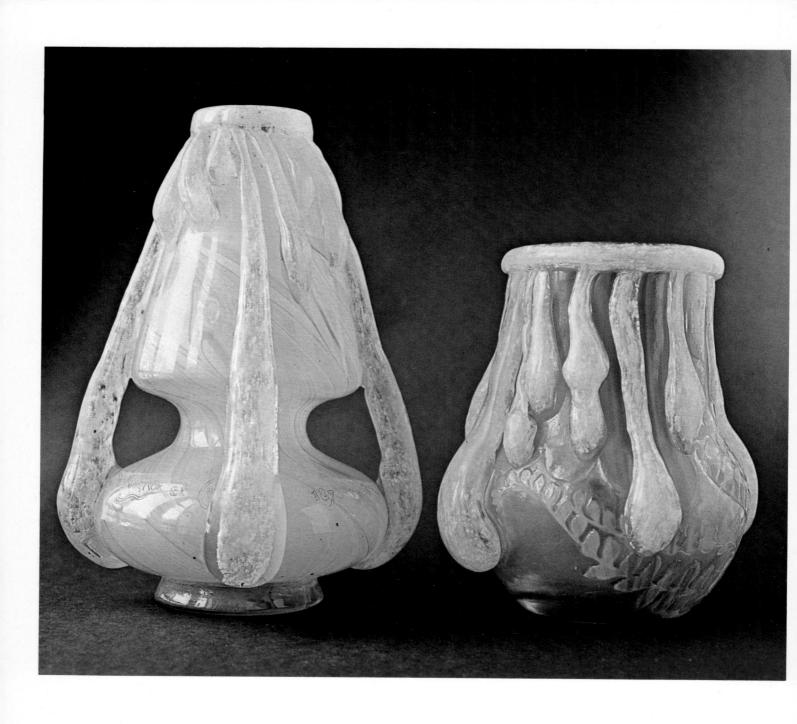

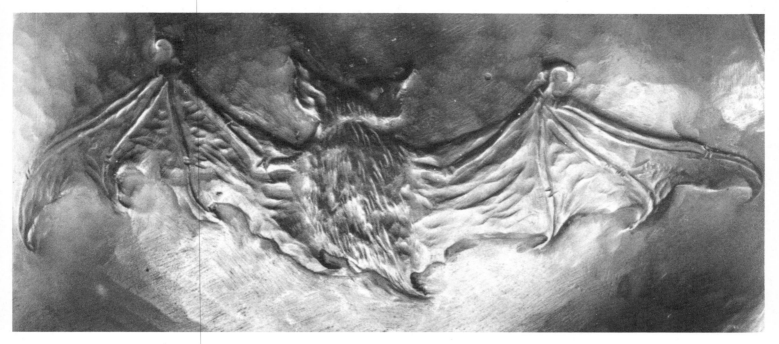

Detail of carved glass vase, 1890s. (Collection Victor Arwas)

Carved scent bottle with internal decoration, 1890s. (Courtesy Maria de Beyrie)

La Chauve-Souris, carved glass flacon, engraved: *'La silence des nuits panse l'âme blessée. La bonté de la nuit caresse l'âme sombre, Emile Gallé del. et ft.'* 1890s. (Collection Mr. and Mrs. Robert Walker)

tions of bizarre winged creatures mingle with those of clouds, with the names of constellations and the tonality of mists.) The bat itself became a prominent symbol in Gallé's iconography and Montesquiou, in turn, would on occasion evoke the qualities of Gallé's glass in his verse. Typical is his description of

> *Un vase de Gallé plein de paillettes mauves,*
> *Baîllant comme un orchis*
> *Un autre parcouru de crépuscules mauves*[25]

As far as Montesquiou could remember his first meeting with Gallé was in 1889. The friendship which developed involved an intensive correspondence and a symbiotic exchange of ideas. Gallé, especially, seemed fired with enthusiasm, and filled with gratitude to this impresario of Beauty whose delicate mind was attuned to the appreciation of the finest works of art or of literature, on the most exquisite scale of values. Gallé, wide-eyed and excited by unexpected intellectual and aesthetic suggestions, wrote to the Count as to a precious guide. He would delight Count Robert by sending letters on wafer-thin strips of veneer or delicately tinted paper adorned with delicate flowers *alla japonica*. The Count was flattered and appreciative: *'Une lettre de (Gallé) est un savant griffonnis, une promenade sur le feuillet, après un préalable bain dans l'encrier, de quelques milliers d'infusoires. Et, parmi, des dessins légers, croquis de buires ou de coupes.'*[25] (A letter from Gallé is a scrawl full of wisdom, a walk taken by a thousand infusoria on the sheet of paper, after a preliminary bathe in the inkwell—and amongst them some slight drawings, some sketches of cups or flagons.) One epistle gave him particular pleasure: *'Je possède de Gallé, un opusculet féerique. La description manuscrite de son envoi de cristaux pour un Salon; chaque page nuancée aux tons du vase décrit, avec un rappel de son décor. Et parmi tant de larmes éclairant le papier de leurs pleurs vitreux, et l'éparpillement aquarellé de brindilles, de folioles, une armée est en marche, un corps de cirons qui sont les caractères trottemenu de la plus fine des écritures.'*[26] (I possess a short but enchanting opuscule by Gallé, the description of his exhibits in crystal for an Exhibition. Each page is imbued with the tints of the vase described and with the memory of its decoration. And amidst so many tears, brightening the pages with their vitreous weeping, amidst the scattering of water-colour sprigs and unfolding leaves, an army is on the match, a regiment of mites—the minute graphic symbols of the most delicate of handwritings.) As well as letters, Gallé sent gifts of plants for the Count's garden at Passy, lilies with their crioceres and other specimens, always with their appropriate parasite.[27] Montesquiou became aware that Gallé was an outstanding botanist and he even showed indulgence to Gallé's drawings, comparing him to Grand-ville, no doubt rather for his imagery than his draughtsmanship.

The association with Montesquiou brought its obvious benefits. There were, of course, the commissions, either for the Count's own satisfaction or as gifts for friends. For the Salon du Champ de Mars of 1892, he commissioned a commode decorated with hydrangeas, the execution of which he supervised very closely. Two years later Montesquiou proposed a cheval-glass on the theme of the wisteria, a piece which was admired by Proust when completed. There is mention, in addition, of a clock case, a huge electuary and a casket, though whether these survive, or were even executed, is uncertain. And, of course, there were the glass vases which the Count found so fascinating and which added to the littered exotica of his homes until his death in 1921.

A second benefit was the number of introductions made as the Count led Gallé through the aesthetic salons of Paris or presented him to other acquaintances. Gallé's encounters with the Comtesse Greffulhe, with the Baroness Adolphe de Rothschild and with Proust were all made possible by Montesquiou. There were others. Count Robert mentions, for example, the occasion on which he first took Gallé, together with Rodin, to Chantilly to meet the Duc d'Aumale[28] and in September 1899 Gallé dedicated to Sarah Bernhardt a carved landscape vase engraved at the top with the line *'de la lumière! de la lumière! Hamlet'*, and with an elaborate engraved dedication *'à Madame Sarah Bernhardt, le grande apôtre de l'Idéal et de la Justice pour l'Art et la Beauté, à la femme de coeur qui en cette forêt de Bondy ne fut ni ne pouvait être du côté des coupe-jarrêts. Gallé Sept. 1899'*.[29] It seems highly probable that it was through the Count that Gallé met her, for the two were old and intimate friends.

Montesquiou sealed his friendship by dedicating certain writings to Gallé. In his anthology of 1893 *Le Chef des Odeurs Suaves* is a poem *Loggia; à Monsieur Emile Gallé*: in the collection *Les Hortensias Bleus* of 1906 the poem *Portenta* is dedicated to Emile Gallé who had noted the particular favour in which the Count held this flower, considering it aristocratic for its lack of scent.[30] Chapter VI of *Les Roseaux Pensants* is dedicated to Gallé, but it is the following chapter, entitled *Orfèvre et Verrier*, which is of particular interest, for it contains a critical appraisal and is probably the most eloquent contemporary vindication of Gallé's work. With an instinctive, and quite understandable, elitism Montesquiou first makes it clear that his interest is exclusively with the *oeuvre d'art* and warns his readers to beware of the *déluge*, the flood of commercial pieces which could possibly mislead them. His concern is with the *véritables vases de Gallé*, those made for Gallé's own satisfaction, according to his own secret formulae, and into which he poured his soul. Montesquiou appreciates the allegories concealed within the colours and contours of such glass, he responds to the symbolism which he describes as 'the intoxicating liquor poured out by the glassmaker in his divine glass'; he shows understanding of the form as well as symbolic significance, enthusing over the chunkiness and the density of glass criticised by some for its heaviness and its lack of delicacy. To level such criticism, he maintained, is to be insensitive to the dignity of this glass, next-of-kin to precious and semi-precious stones. Gallé's work in wood is deliciously detailed in another section of *Les Roseaux Pensants* as the Count invites the reader to examine '. . . *un dessus de table de Gallé; déchiffrez jusqu'au plus tendre quart de soupir, la polyphonique orchestration de cette musique ligneuse. Une nouvelle harmonie en jaillira pour vos yeux, de chaque veine. Un pli de terrain, un cours d'eau; et d'un noeud de bois, un nuage. La marqueterie y concourt . . . On devine, on sait*

Sarah Bernhardt photographed by Downey, 1879. (Private Collection)

Free-form blown glass vase with metallic inclusions in a wrought-iron mount, *c.* 1900. (Collection Félix Marcilhac, Paris)

les aveux qu'un ébéniste ainsi fait, obtient du coeur d'un arbre abattu, et fait raconter aux essences. On dirait que l'histoire de la forêt chante d'elle-même en ces placages nuancés, en ces mosaïques vapoureuses. Il y bouge une ombre mouvante de nue, en reflet d'oiseaux émigrants, et des tons y sont évanouis comme un rêve interrompu de dryade . . .'[31] (A table top by Gallé—decipher it down to the most delicate quaver, this polyphonic orchestration of linear music. From each vein a new harmony will flash to your eyes. A fold of the terrain, a waterway—a knot in the wood becomes a cloud. Marquetry helps in this creation . . . One guesses, one knows, the confessions which such a cabinet maker will obtain from the heart of a felled tree, the tree's very essence talks through him. It seems as if the forest sings its own story through these shaded veneers, these filmy mosaics—There stirs the moving shadow of a cloud, the reflections of migratory birds and fleeting shades like the interrupted dream of some dryad.)

Paul Verlaine. (Radio Times Hulton Picture Library)

The relationship, however, came to grief and, in the pages of his memoirs, it is with malice that Montesquiou details his abandonment of Gallé.[32] He comments dryly on the artist's lack of '. . . that safeguard one calls taste', finds loathsome his proposals of 1889 discussed in the essay *Applications Industrielles. Vulgarisation Artistique*, and accuses Gallé of having, by such commercialisation *'(fait) pipi à l'ésthétique'*. He unkindly describes Gallé's naïve pleasure in inviting him to dinner and decorating the otherwise elegant table with a plant that would have been better suited to the cracks of an old wall, and Gallé's childish delight in revealing that the plant was the *Geranium robertium*. When Montesquiou told this story the first time, in 1897, he had been amused, even flattered by his host's thoughtfulness.[33] The last straw, the incident which determined Montesquiou henceforth to ignore Gallé's letters, he describes[34] as a social blunder which, according to the Count added *'vulgarisation d'amitié'* to *'vulgarisation d'art'*. It was at a party that Gallé inadvertently snubbed his friend by showing more interest in some woman of pseudo-royal Balkan background than in the host, a worthy Duke, a friend to whom the Count wished to introduce Gallé.

As unjust as these last lines from a cynical Montesquiou, but without his malice, was the tribute paid to Gallé by Verlaine. The poet was invited to Nancy for a banquet organised in his honour. Gallé, who was amongst the guests at the banquet, presented him with a delightful vase decorated with clematis, as a token of his esteem. No sooner had Verlaine arrived back in Paris and stepped down from his train, however, than he sold the vase for forty glasses of absinthe.[35]

Conclusion

Le Renouveau, 1890s. (Contemporary photograph)

The potency of Gallé's art is in its honesty. Never does Gallé efface any part of himself or conceal any aspect of his vision. The richness of his art is in the depth of his perception and in the completeness of this vision. It is here that Gallé diverges from traditional Christian standards. In the Christian faith a dividing line is drawn between the power of good and evil, between heaven and hell; a distinction is made between the admissible and the inadmissible. Gallé, however, adopts a pantheism based on a less masochistically moral double standard by accepting the duality of his nature and of his fascinations. Some are frightened by the qualities of certain of Gallé's creations. Surely the fear stems only from their own false sense of self-doubt. Gallé has accepted, and displays in his work, the dual polarity of his soul with its attractions for what might be categorised as the forces of light and of dark. He describes his task as dreaming up for glass '. . . *des roles tendres ou terribles*',[1] soft or savage characters, and he borrows the words of Count Robert de Montesquiou when, in the inscription on the vase *Fiori Oscuri*, he declares '*J'aime l'heure où tout changeant de forme, le clair et l'obscure luttent ensemble*'. Gallé does not moralise; there is no moral to be drawn from this *éternel débât* between light and dark, for it is the quintessential struggle of life. Ultimately, the majority of Gallé's works can be understood in terms of these twin aspects of creation.

He virtually defined them in an exceptional carved glass vase on which he depicted symbolically the *éternel débât*. The struggle is between a savage pterodactyl, carved in bitter brown glass symbolising the forces of darkness, of evil, and a pelican, carved in intaglio into pale whitish glass, a pelican symbolic of the forces of light, of renewal and of good. For the pelican tore at its own breast to feed its young and continue the cycle of life.

Symbols of light abound in Gallé's work, if by light one means the expression of his profound joy in the cycle of life—symbols of evolution and renewal, of birth and rebirth, through the seasons, through the regeneration of plant and animal life and, by analogy, through the three ages and the rebirth of man. Louis de Fourcaud illustrates a sideboard, designed on the theme of the springing up of a wild clematis stem, its flowering and the scattering of its seed so that the process might be eternal. It is titled '*Le Renouveau*', the renewal.[2]

On the flanks of honey-coloured vases, bees hum with activity, as they carry back the germ from pollinating flowers or construct their honey combs, unconsciously working to perpetuate themselves; blindly, instinctively playing their parts in the processes of nature. Elsewhere, spiders spin the webs to catch the stray insects which are their source of sustinence and of life. Certain vases depict the life cycle of a flower, sprouting from the ground, growing, blossoming, and finally, before dying, sowing the seed for its rebirth. In other

Enamelled amber glass bowl, 1890s.
(Sotheby's Belgravia)

instances, the symbol is represented sculpturally, rather than graphically. The vase *L'Oignon* made by Gallé for the Universal Exhibition of 1900 is a fine example of the artist's expression of joy at the process of growth. The foot of the vase, fine, swirling lines of colour drawn in a clear body, represent the beginnings, the actual roots of the onion; the body of the vase is the onion itself, its outer layers peeling away; finally, on the flaring neck flourish the onion-head flowers, reaching up towards the warm, flame-like tongues of rich red glass around the rim. The entire cycle is evoked. *Les Tétards*, a vase first executed in carved cameo glass and then repeated for the 1900 Universal Exhibition in *marqueterie sur verre* and applied glass, represents the growth of the tadpole, traditional symbol of the embryonic state. The spawn flourishes against the pond green glass, splashed with the dark green plankton that is essential as nourishment for this cycle.

The progress of the days and of the seasons is a key element of Gallé's symbolism. The bed *Aube et Crépuscule* embodies the concept of the eternal cycle of the days as well as the quite literal symbolism of light and of dark. For Gallé, the most moving of the seasons was autumn, by its association with the gathering of a year's harvest marking the close of a phase in the cycle. 'Les blancs soleils d'automne'[3] shone for him with particular poignancy. For the Salon des Beaux Arts of 1903 Gallé made a vast sideboard on the theme of autumn and harvest. The panels of the lower doors depict, in marquetry, the gathering of the crop, the newly-piled haystacks, whilst on the *vitrine* above iron snowflakes give threat and warning of impending winter. The two symbols most closely associated by Gallé with the harvest are the wheat and the vine. Many are his applications of the theme of proud stalks laden with corn or of vines laden with bursting grapes. Here are the most elemental symbols of man's sustinence and, as the bread and the wine, the two traditional elements in the ritualistic 'communion' with creation. And, as he offers his gratitude for the bread and the wine, so in turn, Gallé borrows the words of St Francis of Assisi in his thanks for the gift of water, inscribed on *La Source*, 'Loué sois tu Seigneur, à cause de notre soeur l'eau, si utile, humble, précieuse et chaste.'

L'Eternel Débât, carved glass vase, 1890s.
(Collection Jean-Claude Brugnot)

A constant counterbalance to this passion for the cycle of life and of light, is the deep fascination exerted on Gallé by the sombre and mysterious, the

131

frightening and the dark. The melancholy lure of the underworld, the symbols of this dark constitute a significant element in his work. Count Robert de Montesquiou describes a visit to Gallé's private workroom, to the atelier that had so enchanted de Fourcaud, but presents it in an altogether different light. His visit was made on a day when a quite different atmosphere, a more sombre mood emanated from Gallé's precious refuge. Montesquiou describes[4] Gallé's deliberate movements as he leads the way towards the room, rattling a mysterious bunch of keys. Ponderously he unlocks the door which creaks slowly ajar on its hinges, laying open the cabinet of this Bluebeard. Montesquiou interprets the mood of the room as one of almost necrophiliac melancholy, overwhelmed by '. . . *les jupes de vos femmes mortes, les tuniques de vos défuntes muses . . . les défroques pailletées et miracées de vos filles mort-nées, ces buires pleines de vos insomnies, ces lagènes gonflées de vos rêves et de vos peines . . .*' (. . . the skirts of your dead women, the tunics of defunct Muses, the spangled, cast-off clothing of your stillborn daughters, those flagons full of your sleeplessness, those musings swollen with your dreams and sorrows.)

The indulgence in gloom is an undeniable feature of Gallé's art. His *vases*

Marine vase with carved and applied decoration, and surface iridescence, *c.* 1900.
(Collection N. Manoukian)

Carved base of a *'vase de tristesse'*, 1890s.
(Collection Mr. and Mrs. Robert Walker)

Designs for *vases de tristesse*, contemporary
engraving after a drawing by Gallé.

Vases de Tristesse, cased *'hyalite'* glass,
that on the left engraved with lines from
Marceline Desbordes Valmore: *S'il viennent
demander pourquoi ta fantaisie. De cette
couleur sombre attriste un temps d'amour....'*
1890s. (Private Collection, London)

de tristesse, vases of sadness, murky creations in tinted black shades, are a category unto themselves, full of melancholy, ultimate symbols of dark, a symbolism which fills the sad, smoky glass as well as expressing itself through the decoration and destination of each individual piece. The bat, creature that has 'vision' and existence only in spaces in which others are blind, beast whose natural habitat is in the dark and gloomy recesses of caves, evokes the darkest recesses of the artist's soul; to Gallé this creature, with its vicious eyes and claws and the repulsive sleekness of its skin is, surely, the descendant of the pterodactyl, prehistoric combattant in the *éternel débât*.

As veiled in mystery and in darkness as the bat, is another symbol dear to

135

Le Chêne, cameo glass vase, 1890s.
(Sotheby & Co.)

Carved marine vase in *'hyalite'* glass, 1890s.
(Private Collection, London)

Gallé—the black and uncharted fathoms of the sea bed, to the impenetrable depths of which Baudelaire compared the human soul. At the end of the nineteenth century the sea bed was as distant as the planets. Jules Verne's adventure *20,000 Leagues under the Sea,* published in 1870, could still frighten and fascinate. Gallé's marine vases, such as those illustrated by de Fourcaud, *Les Secrets de la Mer,* a *vase flacon* with stopper and *Les Carnivores,* depicting the flesh consuming savages of the sea, constitute a characteristic element of Gallé's involvement with the dark, with a world of extended perceptions into which he constantly yet discreetly lures his audience.

137

The desk, *La Forêt Lorraine*, supporting fine exhibition standard vases, 1901. (Contemporary photograph)

La Forêt Lorraine, 1900 (Sotheby & Co.)

The desk *La Forêt Lorraine* makes a typically discreet invitation to the inner world of the imagination, to the bewitching riches of the mind open to every outside influence and internal pressure. The fall-front desk, of relatively conventional form, has as its structural and decorative theme the Forests of Lorraine. Inlaid in fruitwood is the line adapted from Baudelaire *'forêt Lorraine, tout y parlerait à l'âme en secret sa douce langue natale.'* The overt invocation is to the wonders of the forests of Gallé's native Lorraine. The allusion, however, is more subtle, for the line adapted from Baudelaire is a signal to the cognoscenti. The invocation is not merely to the forests of Lorraine; the invocation is to a world beyond forests into the realms of the imagination, to escape through the forest into fantasy, into a world whose riches derive from the inner resources of man's heart. For the words are borrowed from Baudelaire's *L'Invitation au voyage*, and the invitation is to a land where '. . . *tout n'est qu'ordre et beauté, luxe, calme et volupté'*.[5]

The sense of giddiness, of intoxication, is very powerful and one is seriously tempted to wonder whether for Gallé intercourse with nature did not include the savouring of hallucinatory plants, so frequently does he depict swaying mushrooms, grey *Inocybe geophylla*, *Grisco-lilacina* and others, beckoning with their threat of toxic power, or the dealy hemlock, repulsive yet fascinating. The mushroom is nowhere more potent or suggestive than in Gallé's disturbing masterpiece *Les Coprins*, whose three giant, overpowering mushrooms lay themselves open to numerous interpretations. There is an undeniably sexual quality to this sprouting cluster of *Coprini* but, above all, *Les Coprins* is surely to be seen as an allegory of the three ages of man, as a parable of the development of man's awareness, for, as the mushrooms burst forth, as they develop, so they become more sensuous, more enticing, until ultimately their

Gilt enamelled glass vase with marine weed decoration, 1900. (Sotheby's Belgravia)

form becomes dissipated. The smallest is restrained, self-contained, the second, opening out, ripening in colour, has a greater tactile interest, whilst the third, fully developed, has acquired a final, blood-red richness and its luscious, swollen, crenellated rim is the colour and texture of flesh.

And, above all, there recurs the poppy flower, *papaver somniferum*, the sleep-inducing poppy, and its opium-bearing pod, the elegant silhouettes of whose fruit acquired for Gallé the symbolism of '. . . *des idées de calme, d'apaisement, de repos*'. An exceptional vase[6] would seem to corroborate the suggestion of indulgence in the use of certain drugs. Cased in a cloudy grey glass, the vase is elaborately carved with whiffs of smoke and bears the engraved intimacy '*Nous étions trois fumeurs, fumant nos pensées, nous étions trois flâneurs, flânant au ciel profond.*' (We were three smokers, smoking our thoughts, we were three drifters, drifting in the endless sky.)

To search in Gallé's work for a message, for a conclusion, is to no avail, for any course of study, any theory pursued returns ultimately to its source, to the elemental root of Gallé's creation—life itself. There is no explanation; one may only feel and interpret. Through his art Gallé is suggesting a new awareness of life, his art being merely the crude approximation of an ideal that has its true existence in the souls of men. Gallé himself quoted Maurice Boucher: '*Dans le grossier symbole éclate l'idéal*'.[7]

Carved cameo mushroom vase with internal decoration, 1890s. (Private Collection, London)

141

Etched, carved and applied glass pot with silver mount and cover, 1890s. (Sotheby's Belgravia)

Silver-mounted, enamelled amber glass vase, 1890s. (Sotheby's Belgravia)

Above right
Cameo glass incense burner with silvered metal mount, *c.* 1900. (Philip Son & Neale)

Watercolour design for three vases including *La Source* (lower), from the Gallé atelier, *c.* 1900. (Collection Lady Abdy)

Cased glass pitcher on the theme of the vine, *c.* 1900. (Private Collection, London)

If one were to admit a didactic quality in Gallé's work, then it would be the preaching of true passion, not of a false social passion, but of a deep spiritual passion, welcomed and nurtured, the preaching of self-understanding and self-acceptance through an appreciation of one's role, at once microscopic and microcosmic, in the progress of the universe. Gallé bares his soul so that others might face their own, and the language which he adopts for this purpose is the richest, the most complex, and yet the most simple of all, for it is a language whose dictionary is in all of our hearts—the language of nature and of life itself. If, for many reasons, Gallé's art appears esoteric, then the only retort is this—that the fault lies not with the artist but with those who observe but do not perceive, whose eyes look but cannot see for their hearts are closed.

Marqueterie sur verre glass flacon, *c.* 1900. (Private Collection, London)

144

Vitrine. (Contemporary photograph)

Detail of a *vitrine,* 1890s. (Courtesy Maria de Beyrie)

Gallé did not hide beneath the cloak of esotericism; nor was he willing to be trite so that the foolish as well as the deserving might claim the keys to his work. These keys exist in an empathy with his use of symbols, a shared feeling for the symbolism which is inspired in him, symbolism of abstract form as well as of colour, texture and line drawn from nature.

> *Tous les objets ont des contours;*
> *Mais d'où vient la forme qui touche?*[8]

Gallé asks an impossible question. All objects have a defining contour, yet from where come those shapes with the power to move men? The answer lies within the question itself—such forms issue from the hearts of men and need no further justification. Gallé states quite categorically that it is in no way desirable for a symbol to be enigmatic.[9] What is important is that the symbol should have feeling, that it have the warmth of human interpretation. There is no symbolism to be found in the coldly analytical pages of a botanical journal. Symbolism emerges only when the artist develops and transfigures his own feelings, as he applies himself to the task, not merely of reproducing flower, insect, landscape or human subject, but of extracting the character and the feeling within. The scientist might argue that the weeping willow sheds no more tears than any other species of willow. Yet to the sensitive it is the sad-

Detail of *vitrine.* (Musée de l'Ecole de Nancy)

Bronze and glass table lamp, 1900. (Maître Georges Blache)

Nous étions trois fumeurs, enamelled glass vase, 1890s. (Collection Jean-Claude Brugnot)

Gilt-bronze mounted blown glass lamp, *c.* 1900. (Collection Alain Lesieutre)

dest of trees. Are roses any more capable of loving than, say, peonies, he might ask. Yet what open heart is not moved by the warmth of roses. It is the magic of human interpretation that causes the transfiguration of decorative motifs into symbols. And their purpose, ultimately, is simple. The function of art, of beauty, or of flowers is, quite simply, to open the hearts of men, '*Pour adoucir les hommes*'.[10] No work that is human can escape being symbolist. To banish symbol from art would, Gallé tells us, be to banish our satellite from the firmament; it would be to deprive of light the morning and evening stars. To banish symbol would be to banish the heavenly bodies which see the open souls of men. It would be to banish creation from art, and this, surely, is not possible.

As the flickering light of the setting sun played on the vases in the depths of Gallé's atelier, setting them aflame with the sparkle of fire or of tears, so the room became for Montesquiou a brazier of precious stones, a brazier in which was consumed only to be eternally reborn, the phoenix of Gallé's creation, '. . . . *l'oiseau fabuleux de (ses) féeries*'.[11] The fire of his dream was, for Gallé, the driving force, and his dream was for reconciliation with the entity of creation, embracing light and dark, clarity and mystery, melancholy and joy. It was a passion born only of love, '*Car amour de l'oeuvre, amour de la nature, amour de son rêve, ne sont que des modes variés de l'infaillible sortilège : aimer.*'[12] (Because love of work, love of nature, love of his dream, are nothing but different manifestations of the inevitable: to love.)

Les Coprins, blown glass lamp of between two and five layers with metallic foil inclusions and iridescent surface effects, in a wrought-iron base, 1904. (Collection Mr. and Mrs. Robert Walker)

Page 152
Carved cased glass *vases d'automne,* 1890s. (Collection Alain Lesieutre)

Inlaid wood signature on a table, 1890s. (Sotheby's Belgravia)

Le Décor Symbolique

Discours de Réception, prononcé à l'Académie de Sta-
nislas, dans la séance publique du 17 mai 1900 et imprimé
dans les Mémoires de cette Compagnie, au tome XVII de
la 5ᵉ série. Émile Gallé avait été élu membre de l'Académie
de Stanislas en 1891.

Dans l'instant où je viens remercier l'Académie de Stanislas
de l'honneur qu'elle me fait par une admission publique, je
pèse avec inquiétude ma dette envers votre hospitalité:
bientôt dix années! Mes créanciers ne se sont pas montrés
trop rigoureux envers la parcimonie de ma constribution à
leurs travaux. Et je sais trop bien votre longanimité, comme
l'insuffisance de mes titres à vos faveurs.

Ces délais, tolérés par vous bonnement, me privent
aujourd'hui d'une joie. Je ne vois pas ici les deux amis qui
furent mes garants auprès de vous; M. Jules Lejeune et le
pasteur Othon Cuvier ne sont plus des nôtres. Si j'évoque
ces deux nobles figures, ce n'est pas par vanité, au moins;
mais je n'ignore pas qu'en accueillant un artisan trop su-
perficiel en des essais divers, vous avez fait crédit surtout au
sentiment de ces deux hommes vénérés, exemplaires l'un et
l'autre par la lumière de leur charité, par leur tolérance
pour toute sincère conviction, et leur sainte ardeur à unir
les hommes dans l'estime, l'étude et la paix. Ils n'eurent
qu'à endormir un peu mes raisons de douter, non de votre
bienveillance, mais de moi-même. Car ma piété envers
notre Académie est née au temps lointain de ma jeunesse,
au grand jour des séances annuelles, à ces antiques et bons
jeudis de mai où mes condisciples du lycée de Nancy, Hubert
Zaepfell et l'angélique Paul Seigneret, le jeune martyr, deux
pures victimes, nous prenaient aux joies bruyantes du cours
Léopold pour venir écouter, dans ce décor royal, les
Lacroix, les Margerie, les Burnouf, les Benoît, les Godron,
les Lombard, les Volland, les Duchêne.

Nos humanités toutes fraîches savouraient le régal d'une
science aimable, d'un atticisme joli comme les guipures
dorées de Jean Lamour. Qui eût pensé que le médiocre
élève des meilleurs maîtres qui fussent oserait un jour, ici,
et, Dieu merci, devant plusieurs d'entre eux, une dis-
sertation française attardée?

Ce devoir trouvera, je l'espère, plus aisément grâce par
le choix d'un sujet familier à mon travail habituel. Ce sera
plus sincère et moins dénué d'intérêt, peut-être.

C'est donc à un compositeur ornemaniste, à un assem-
bleur d'images que vous voulez bien cette fois donner la
parole, pour vous parler du symbolisme dans le décor.

* * *

Imaginer des thèmes propres à revêtir de lignes, de
formes, de nuances, de pensées, les parements de nos
demeures et les objets d'utilité ou de pur agrément, adapter
son dessein aux moyens d'élaboration propres à chaque
matière, métal ou bois, marbre ou tissu, cela est une occupation absorbante, certes. Mais elle est plus sérieuse au fond,
plus grave de conséquences, que le compositeur d'orne-
ments ne le coupçonne d'habitude.

Toute mise en action de l'effort humain, si infime que,
souvent, le résultat paraisse, se résume dans le geste du
semeur, geste redoutable parfois. Or, inconsidérément ou
de propos délibéré, le dessinateur, lui aussi, fait oeuvre de
semeur. Il ensemence un champ dévolu à une culture
spéciale, le décor, à des outils, à des ouvriers, à des
germes, à des récoltes déterminées. Car, parmi les orne-
ments qui naissent de ses préoccupations habituelles, les
plus humbles comme les plus exaltés peuvent devenir un
jour des éléments dans cet ensemble documentaire révé-
lateur: *le style décoratif d'une époque.* En effet, toute
création d'art est conçue et naît sous les influences, parmi
les ambiances des songeries et des volitions les plus coutu-
mières de l'artiste. C'est de là, quoi qu'il en ait, que surgit
son ouvrage. Qu'il y consente ou non, ses préoccupations
sont au nouveau-né des marraines, bonne fées ou sor-
cières, qui jettent des mauvais sorts ou confèrent des dons
magiques. L'œuvre portera la marque indélébile d'une
cogitation, d'une habitude passionnée de l'esprit. Elle
synthétisera un symbole, inconscient, et d'autant plus
profond. — Certains tapis d'Asie sont marqués, parmi la
trame et les laines, d'une soyeuse mèche de cheveux de
femme; c'est la marque personnelle de la tâche accomplie.

Tel un livre clos laisse voir, au ruban fané, la page méditée, préférée, parfois à jamais interrompue. Ainsi le décorateur mêle à son ouvrage quelque chose de lui. Plus tard on démêlera l'écheveau; on retrouvera le cheveu blanchi, la larme essuyée, — les autographes de Marceline Valmore en sont illisibles souvent, — et la chose muette exhalera ou bien le soupir de lassitude et de dégoût pour la tâche non volontaire et rebutante, ou bien le viril satisfecit du poète:

> O soir, aimable soir, désiré par celui
> Dont les bras, sans mentir, peuvent dire: Aujourd'hui
> Nous avons travaillé!

On ignore le nom du bel artiste penseur, statuaire d'Égypte, orfèvre royal, mage, ou décorateur de temples, qui, s'étant arrêté à contempler le manège d'un fangeux insecte, le bousier stercoraire, pétrissant une boule de fumier pour y déposer ses œufs dans la chaleur du sable libyque, fut ému d'un respect religieux. Il sut le premier, par delà les apparences, découvrir le reflet d'une image auguste, inventer ce joyau mystique, *le scarabée sacré*. De ses pattes antérieures, — et plus tard dans les imitations phéniciennes, de ses ailes éployées, — l'insecte soutient le globe solaire, foyer de la lumière, de la chaleur; dans ses pattes postérieures il roule maternellement un autre corps céleste, un globe, la terre, où il dépose les germes de la vie. Quel témoignage, rendu par l'inventeur artiste, à l'existence d'un Dieu créateur, à la providentielle mise au point du satellite avec la source du calorique! Étrange et très antique prescience, dirait-on, de la forme planétaire terrestre elle-même: voilà un symbole artistique, cosmographique, religieux et divinateur. Mais ce qu'atteste surtout, chez l'artiste, une telle invention, c'est une qualité d'âme et de pensée habituelle d'une surprenante et prophétique beauté.

Cet exemple caractéristique me permet de vous épargner les définitions plus ou moins rébarbatives qu'on a données du symbole, du symbolisme et de l'art symbolique. Nous entendons bien, n'est-ce pas? que le symbole dans les domaines divers de l'art, de la poésie, de la religion, c'est *la figuration d'une chose*, *abstraite le plus souvent*, *figuration conventionnelle*, *signe convenu entre initiés*; c'est, dans le décor, dans le vase comme dans la médaille, la statue, le tableau, le bas-relief, le temple, aussi bien que dans le poème, l'œuvre chantée ou mimée, — c'est toujours la traduction, l'éveil d'une idée par une image.

> Dans le grossier symbole éclate l'idéal,

dit Maurice Bouchor. Et le décor symbolique s'accommode humblement de cette définition: à lui toute figure ornementale, toute synthèse du dessin, de la plastique, de la nuance, propres à rendre les abstractions les plus subtiles; à condition qu'il soit un peu poète, il a carte blanche; car le poète est le symboliste par excellence. Comment le décorateur s'y prendra-t-il donc? — Un peu comme Bernardin de Saint-Pierre: "J'apportai un bouton

de rose avec ses épines, comme le symbole de mes espérances, mêlées de beaucoup de craintes."

Mais il est désirable que le symbole ne soit pas trop énigmatique; l'esprit de France aime la clarté; il a raison; car, dit Hugo,

> L'idée à qui tout cède est toujours claire.

Et le spectateur français, devant les modernes florilèges britanniques, qui sont parfois de véritables charades fleuries, se pique de pouvoir à la fin, comme Victor Hugo, déchiffrer le rébus:

> Une rose me dit: Devine!
> Et je lui répondis: Amour!

Est-ce à dire que la rose soit plus amoureuse que la pivoine? "Le saule pleureur, dit un esthéticien, Lévêque, dans sa *Science du beau*, ne pleure point davantage que les autres saules; la violette n'est pas plus modeste que le pavot." L'expression morale des végétaux est donc purement symbolique. Concitoyens d'un des plus délicieux symbolistes, Grandville, nous avons appris à lire dans ses *Fleurs animées* et ses *Étoiles*; et nous savons bien que cette éloquence de la fleur, grâce aux mystères de son organisme et de sa destinée, grâce à la synthèse du symbole végétal sous le crayon de l'artiste, dépasse parfois en intense pouvoir suggestif l'autorité de la figure humaine. Nous savons que l'expression, dans notre chardon héraldique par exemple, tient au geste braveur, et, dans d'autres plantes, à l'air penché, à la ligne pensive, à la nuance emblématique, et que nuances, galbes, parfums, sont des vocables de ce que Baudelaire appelait:

> Le langage des fleurs et des choses muettes.

* * *

Ici se présente une question: Quelle est la qualité décorative du symbole? Pour nous servir d'un mot de métier, le symbole dans l'ornement est-il *meublant?* Le symboliste ne sacrifiera-t-il pas le plaisir des yeux à des jeux de l'esprit? Il est certain que le signe symbolique de la plus noble idée ne fera pas une tache plus décorative que toute banale rosace, s'il n'est pas vivifié par l'accent du dessin, par la mise en valeur, et puissance du simulacre, au moyen des prestiges du relief ou du coloris. Il n'est pas moins évident que ce n'est point l'emploi du symbole qui pourra conférer magiquement des grâces si spéciales à un décor sans métier et sans génie.

Mais qui ne conçoit que l'artiste, penché à reproduire la fleur, l'insecte, le paysage, la figure humaine, et qui cherche à en extraire le caractère, le sentiment contenu, fera une œuvre plus vibrante et d'une émotion plus contagieuse que celui dont l'outil ne sera qu'un appareil photo-

Cameo glass vase, detail. (Collection Alain
Lesieutre)

graphique, ou qu'un froid scalpel? Le document naturaliste le plus scrupuleux, reproduit dans un ouvrage scientifique, ne nous émeut pas, parce que l'âme humaine en est absente; tandis que la reproduction, cependant très naturelle de l'artiste japonais, par exemple, sait traduire d'une façon unique le motif évocateur, ou le minois tantôt moqueur, tantôt mélancolique de l'être vivant, de la chose pensive. Il en fait inconsciemment, par sa seule passion pour la nature, de véritables symboles de la *Forêt*, de la *Joie du printemps*, des *Tristesses de l'automne*. Ainsi donc, dans l'ornement, le symbole est un point lumineux parmi l'insignifiance paisible et voulue des rinceaux et des arabesques; le symbole pique l'attention; c'est lui qui fait entrer en scène la pensée, la poésie et l'art. Les symboles sont les pointes où se concrètent les idées.

Mais d'ailleurs, disons-le, il serait bien inutile de déconseiller au décorateur l'emploi du symbole, qui est si volontiers accepté chez le poète. Et, tant que la pensée guidera la plume, le pinceau, le crayon, il ne faut pas douter que le symbole ne continue de charmer les hommes. D'ailleurs, l'amour de la nature ramènera toujours le symbolisme: la fleur aimée de tous, populaire, jouera toujours dans l'ornement un rôle principal et symbolique. Gutskow raconte qu'un chercheur du vrai bonheur, ayant interrogé la fleur, celle-ci l'avait renvoyé à l'étoile. A son tour l'astre répondit à l'homme: "Retourne bien vite au bleuet."

Pas plus que les poètes, — les joailliers, les dentellières ne sauraient se passer de la nature. C'est *leur droit* à tous, c'est *leur domaine*, c'est *la source vive!* Victor Hugo l'avoue, lui, le grand agitateur de symboles:

> Nous ne ferions rien qui vaille
> Sans l'orme et sans le houx,
> Et l'oiseau travaille
> A nos poèmes avec nous.

Calderon rend à la fleur cet hommage: "Si ma voix est nouvelle, si j'ai reçu un nouveau cœur, c'est à la fleur que je dois mon renouveau!" Et pour lui la fleur devenait le symbole de la réconciliation avec la beauté morale, avec la divinité.

Pour bannir le symbole du décor, il faudrait chasser du firmament notre satellite:

> Cette faucille d'or dans le champ des étoiles!

Il faudrait éteindre "l'étoile du matin et l'étoile du soir", il faudrait effacer ces apostrophes, les constellations. Pour que le symbole se taise à jamais dans l'art, il faudrait effacer "Dieu, l'astre sacré que voit l'âme"; car, au fond, le mot de toute la nature, de règne en règne, de symbole en symbole, de reflet en reflet,

> Le mot, c'est Dieu:
> Les constellations le disent au silence!

Et voilà justement ce qui a fait la force de notre art national, depuis ses manifestations primitives, jusqu'au geste émouvant qui élance vers le ciel la prière de nos cathédrales. Voilà ce qui a fait sa beauté dans sa verte expansion du treizième siècle: c'est qu'il ne s'enfermait pas dans l'atelier; comme le lierre au tronc du chêne, il se cramponnait à la libre nature, c'est-à-dire au symbolisme même. Baudelaire a formulé d'une façon grandiose cette conception des résonances harmoniques en l'immense création:

> La Nature est un temple, où de vivants piliers
> Laissent parfois sortir de confuses paroles.
> L'homme y passe à travers des forêts de symboles,
> Qui l'observent avec des regards familiers.

C'est là toute l'histoire de notre décor national celtique, gaulois, fier enfant de la rude nature, fils des druides, des bardes, revenant toujours, après toutes les invasions, celles du Midi et celles de l'Est, après tous les mélanges, toutes les modes, romaines ou barbares, à sa nature, la Nature, à son génie libre, à ses sources, la flore et la faune indigènes, à la joie de l'ouvrier d'orner son œuvre librement à son foyer, à son goût, amoureusement. Et ainsi, notre décor populaire, symboliste sans le savoir, comme la nature elle-même, comme le chêne vert et la lande, va des fougeraies de Gavr'innis aux bronzes fleuronnés de Basançon, aux poteries feuillagées de la Champagne, puis aux lierres et aux vignes de ces délicates œuvres gallo-grecques, concédez-moi ce néologisme en faveur des produits attiques de nos vieilles officines de la Marne, de l'Allier, du Rhône, au quatrième siècle. L'esprit de terroir se formulait alors en joyeux souhaits sur les gobelets parlants de Reims et de Vichy, qui se souvenaient des calices devisants de la Grèce, et faisaient présager notre gaillarde faïence gauloise des seizième et dix-huitième siècles. De même nos repentirs contemporains vers l'art décoratif sont des retours heureux à la Brocéliande, à la forêt celtique, comme l'ont été les glorieuses frondaisons nationales des treizième et seizième siècles.

Car c'est bien l'antique poterie des Gaules qui, dans les "rustiques figulines" de Bernard Palissy, réapparaît, se moule étroitement sur la nature comme une empreinte fossile, se revêt de couleurs vraies, mouillant les objets d'un liquide émail; c'est elle qui précise, dans des reproductions vivantes, les caractères spécifiques des frondes de nos diverses fougères, et, au bord des eaux douces endormies ou des eaux courantes, les caractères de nos coquilles palustres ou fluviales, de nos crustacés et de nos poissons. — Oui, nous savons qu'il a été naguère de bon ton de rabaisser, en de certaines chaires à paradoxes, en de certaines chapelles à préjugés, l'*Art utilitaire*, et les ouvrages de nos vieux métiers. Saisissons au passage cette occasion-ci de proclamer *le principe de l'unité de l'art*, en rendant hommage au fier ancêtre, à l'un des patrons des arts français du feu, au symboliste de "l'art de terre". Et il suffit, pour lui rendre justice, de rappeler quelle fut la qualité des préoccupations d'où sortirent ses argiles vives, et l'invention française,

Glass vase with applied *marqueterie* and
internal decoration, *c.* 1900. (Collection
Félix Marcilhac, Paris)

gauloise, des couvertes limpides. Laissons-le dire lui-même quel fut son dessein, son but:

"Quelques jours après que les émotions et les guerres civiles furent apaisées, et qu'il eut plu à Dieu de nous envoyer sa paix, j'étais un jour me promener le long de la prairie de cette ville de Saintes, près du fleuve de Charente. Et tandis que je contemplais les horribles dangers desquels Dieu m'avait garanti au temps des tumultes passés, j'ouïs la voix de certaines jeunes filles assises dans les saussaies et qui chantaient le psaume CIV. Et parc que leurs voix étaient douces et bien accordantes, cela me fit oublier mes premières pensées, et, m'étant arrêté pour écouter ledit psaume, je laissai le plaisir des voix et entrai en contemplation sur le sens. Et dis en moi-même: Admirable bonté de Dieu! Mon dessein serait que nous eussions les oeuvres de tes mains en telle révérence comme David en ce psaume. Et dès lors je pensai d'édifier un jardin conforme au dessin, ornement et excellente beauté de ce que le prophète a décrit dans ce psaume, un amphithéâtre de refuge qui serait une sainte délectation et honnête occupation de corps et d'esprit."

Ainsi donc, voilà le mystère de toute cette "con-chyliologie qui ennuya Bouvard et Pécuchet" et nous valut cette boutade pédantesque d'un de nos modernes critiques français (Brunetière) à propos des ouvrages de Palissy: "Il n'y a pas d'art dans un pot, parce qu'il n'y a pas de dessein", c'est-à-dire de préméditation. Or, ce fut chez le potier de Saintes un dessein, un véritable voeu d'initier les hommes, par des reproductions de la nature, à voir Dieu à travers les similitudes et les beautés de ses œuvres les plus humbles.

* * *

A son tour, le décorateur moderne aura-t-il assez de sincérité, de foi, pour qu'il fasse jaillir de son œuvre une symbolique rajeunie, un art libre, en réalisant au travers et au moyen d'une constante scrutation de la nature, le progrès et l'idéal meilleur et plus haut qui ont droit de compter parmi les préoccupations habituelles d'un artiste?

Et d'abord, la nature lui apporte aujourd'hui des formes nouvelles; la science lui offre des symboles vierges, carac-téristiques, inconnus à nos ancêtres et propres à frapper les regards qui ont désappris de voir les choses familières. Dans la circulation des idées et l'échange de nos officines décoratives actuelles, on voit déjà passer aujourd'hui la *parmentière*, cette bonne solanée, la *paradisie alpestre* ou *lis de Saint-Bruno*, les *dictames*, les *Malvacées*, le *diélytra*, introduit depuis le commencement du siècle, et qui, par sa forme cordée, si élégante et si suggestive, par ses tendres coloris, par le pli ailé de ses deux pétales externes, s'imposera aujourd'hui comme un symbole d'amour et de cordialité; la fleur à la corolle caractéristique, turbinée; la *pervenche*, la *parisette*, d'une douteuse bonne foi; et la *douce-amère*, de l'illustre famille des bonnes empoison-neuses, cette sœur des poisons, ou plutôt des remèdes intenses: la *jusquiame*, la *belladone*, la *mandragore*; la

douce-amère, quel touchant emblème! C'est la saveur de la douleur féconde, de l'épreuve salutaire, c'est l'emblème des consciences inquiètes.

Nous avouons des préférences pour les bonnes vieilles plantes, chères à nos aïeules. Mais le rapide courant moderne est plus profond, plus puissant que le ruisseau paisible de nos prédilections. Il emporte tout. Il nous jette — comme un dernier bouquet d'Ophélie — l'orchidée, avec une richesse, une étrangeté inconcevable de formes, d'espèces, de parfums, de coloris, de caprices, de voluptés et d'inquiétants mystères.

Enfin, la science, de tous les côtés, ouvre au décorateur des horizons nouveaux. L'océanographie, qui a parmi nous à Nancy l'un de ses plus passionnés adeptes, est comme le magicien plongeur dans les contes des *Mille et une Nuits*, le roi de la mer, qui emporte dans ses bras ses favoris terrestres pour leur faire visiter les palais bleus:

> Homme libre, toujours tu chériras la mer.
> La mer est ton miroir, tu contemples ton âme.
> Vous êtes tous les deux ténébreux et discrets.
> Homme! nul n'a sondé le fond de tes abîmes.
> O mer! nul ne connaît tes richesses intimes,
> Tant vous êtes jaloux de garder vos secrets.
>
> *Baudelaire.*

Ces secrets de l'Océan, les braves sondeurs nous les livrent. Ils vident des récoltes marines qui, des laboratoires, font des ateliers d'art décoratif, des musées de modèles. Ils dessinent, ils publient pour l'artiste ces matériaux in-soupçonnés, les émaux et les camées de la mer. Bientôt les méduses cristallines insuffleront des nuances et des galbes inédits aux calices des verres.

Ainsi pour trouver, à côté des formes et des décors nouveaux, les symboles d'un art neuf, il suffira de regarder autour de soi, de chercher à savoir, d'étudier et d'aimer; car le symbole jaillira spontanément chez le décorateur de ces forces combinées: l'étude de la nature, l'amour de son art et le besoin d'exprimer ce qu'on a dans le coeur.

C'est là ce qu'a trop souvent oublié l'artiste du dix-neuvième siècle. Cet âge, surprenant, admirable à tant d'égards, a prétendu produire du décor, en inonder in-dustriellement et commercialement le monde, et cela dans des conditions bien spéciales, bien fâcheuses; les exécutants de ces décors actuels n'ont guère pu, comme leurs ancêtres, apprécier la pure joie de l'ouvrier amoureux de son œuvre; le compositeur lui-même s'est traîné dans de serviles imita-tions du passé, copies dont la pensée était absente, dont le symbole, créé par d'autres âges, est incompris du nôtre, et répond à d'autres besoins, à une autre conception de la vie.

Ceci fut une des erreurs, l'une des peines amères de l'âge de l'industrialisme, de la division outrée du travail, de son organisation loin du foyer domestique, de la famille et de ses naturelles ambiances, dans une atmosphère empoisonnée, artificielle. Le siècle qui va finir n'a pas eu d'art populaire, c'est-à-dire d'art appliqué aux objets d'utilité et exécuté spontanément, joyeusement par les artisans eux-mêmes à leurs métiers; et ce sont les mieux informés de nos contemporains, les plus généreux esprits, les plus laborieux et les plus nobles artistes qui ont fait cette constatation.

Mais saluons le retour à une meilleure conception du labeur. William Morris, ce grand artiste, ce philosophe humanitaire, ce prophète de la joie au travail, a dit que le labeur est humain, qu'il est bon, que l'art est salutaire; que l'art béni, sauveur, c'est l'art populaire, c'est-à-dire l'expression de la joie de l'homme dans le travail des choses.

Et nous pouvons proclamer à notre tour notre foi profonde en la doctrine qui assigne à l'art une fonction de culture humaine, d'éveil des esprits et des âmes par la traduction des beautés épandues dans le monde.

De si hautes visées sont-elles interdites à l'art? Qui l'oserait soutenir devant les calligraphies paradisiaques de l'Alhambra, les loges du Vatican, les lambris de la Sixtine, les allégories pleines de bonhomie, de simplicité, de douceur et d'amour, l'art symbolique et suave, l'art chrétien des deuxième et troisième siècles, au cimetière de Saint-Calixte? N'est-ce point précisément parce que le symbole vit et vibre dans ces œuvres d'élite qu'elles ont sur les âmes une si mystérieuse action? C'est aussi le décor tel que l'a réalisé Puvis de Chavannes.

Une femme très âgée, émaciée par les veilles, les sacrifices de toute une vie de piété et de pitié, un corps que soutient seul et dresse debout une ardente charité, s'appuie avec une sollicitude auguste sur le balcon d'une terrasse. La nuit est avancée. Les étoiles pâlissent. La ville dort. C'est son enfant, à cette femme. C'est une inquiétude maternelle pour la cité qui l'a forcée à se lever, qui la cloue à sa place dans le froid du matin.

Sainte Geneviève craint pour sa Lutèce l'incendie, les Huns au dehors, l'ennemi au dedans. Paris, tu peux dormir. Geneviève écoute dans le silence profond. Sa lampe veille aussi et sa main se pose sur la pierre comme si elle redoutait d'éveiller un nouveau-né. Cette ombre d'aïeule est le symbole même de l'amour. Cette lampe est le symbole de l'âme éveillée. Ce silence qui émane de l'œuvre et se pose à l'entour, chacun l'emporte dans son cœur.

Laissez-moi m'arrêter après cet exemple admirable du plus pur symbole.

Ma conclusion est donc que le terme de *symbole* est bien près de se confondre avec celui d'*art*. Concient ou inconscient, le symbole qualifie, vivifie l'œuvre; il en est l'âme. Et à l'aube du vingtième siècle, il est permis de saluer le renouveau d'un art national populaire, annonciateur de temps meilleurs. — "C'est l'œuvre de l'artiste moderne, a dit Charles Albert au Congrès pour l'art à Bruxelles, qui créera l'atmosphère de demain." Elle doit être, cette œuvre, une lutte pour la Justice en nous-mêmes, pour la Justice autour de nous. Et ainsi la vie au vingtième siècle ne devra plus manquer de joie, d'art, ni de beauté.

Notes to the Text

Chapter 1
1. *Art et Décoration*, July-December 1911, p. 235
2. *The Studio*, Vol. XXVIII, pp. 108-117

Chapter 2
1. *Ecrits pour l'Art*, pp. 237-238
2. *Ecrits pour l'Art*, p. 239
3. *Art et Décoration*, July-December 1911, p. 238, footnote
4. *Ecrits pour l'Art*, pp. 148-154
5. De Fourcaud, p. 38
6. De Fourcaud, p. 39
7. *Art et Industrie*, July 1909

Chapter 3
1. *Ecrits pour l'Art*, pp. 22-23
2. *Ecrits pour l'Art*, p. 54
3. *Ecrits pour l'Art*, p. 77
4. *Ecrits pour l'Art*, p. 81
5. *Ecrits pour l'Art*, p. 102
6. *Ecrits pour l'Art*, pp. 59-60
7. *Ecrits pour l'Art*, pp. 157-158
8. De Fourcaud, p. 38
9. De Fourcaud, p. 47
10. *Ecrits pour l'Art*, p. 133
11. *Gazette des Beaux Arts*, May-June 1963, p. 370
12. De Fourcaud, p. 41
13. De Fourcaud, p. 36
14. *The Magazine of Art*, March 1897, p. 250

Chapter 4
1. *Art et Décoration*, July-December 1911, pp. 238-240
2. *Art et Décoration*, July-December 1905, p. 102
3. *Ecrits pour l'Art*, p. 301
4. *Ecrits pour l'Art*, p. 319
5. *Art et Décoration*, July-December 1911, p. 239
6. *Ecrits pour l'Art*, p. 119

Chapter 5
1. *Ecrits pour l'Art*, p. 355
2. *Ecrits pour l'Art*, p. 264
3. *Ecrits pour l'Art*, p. 365
4. *Ecrits pour l'Art*, p. 240
5. *Ecrits pour l'Art*, p. 251
6. *Revue des Arts Décoratifs*, Vol. XII, pp. 381-383
7. *Apollo*, August 1972, p. 131
8. *Art et Décoration*, January-June 1898, p. 110
9. Christie's sale catalogue, 2 November 1971, Lot 53, footnote
10. Published in part in Maurice Rheims, *The Age of Art Nouveau*, pp. 230-231
11. *Art et Décoration*, July-December 1911, p. 245
12. De Fourcaud, p. 61
13. The description is from Baudelaire's dedication to Gautier
14. *The Artist*, 1900, p. 9
15. De Fourcaud, p. 62
16. De Fourcaud, p. 51

Chapter 6
1. Et seq. De Fourcaud, pp. 35-36
2. See *Glass Magazine*, November-December 1972, pp. 29-32
3. Richard Dennis, "The Glass of Emile Gallé", *Antiques International*, 1967, p. 183
4. Et seq. *Ecrits pour l'Art*, pp. 332-353
5. From a verse by Sully Prudhomme
6. Private Collection, London
7. *Ecrits pour l'Art*, pp. 348-349
8. *Gazette des Beaux Arts*, May-June 1963, p. 374, note 21
9. Et seq. *La Nature*, 1 March 1913, pp. 209-212

Chapter 7
1. *Magazine of Art*, March 1897, p. 249
2. *Magazine of Art*, March 1897, p. 252
3. De Fourcaud, p. 14

4. De Fourcaud, p. 13
5. *Journal* for Wednesday 26 June 1895
6. *Ecrits pour l'Art*, p. 75
7. Conserved in Paris among family archives
8. *The Architectural Record*, Vol. 13, March 1903, p. 278
9. *Art et Décoration*, July-December 1911, p. 234
10. *L'Art Décoratif*, March 1905, p. 131
11. The story is told in a long letter from Proust to Antoine Bibesco on the occasion of his mother's death. *Cahiers Marcel Proust, 2*, pp. 55-56
12. Et seq. *Contre Ste Beuve*, pp. 513 and 444
13. *Lettre à Robert de Billy, Lettres et Conversations*, pp. 31-33
14. *Contre Ste Beuve*, p. 88
15. *Le Côté de Guermantes*, p. 392
16. *A l'Ombre des Jeunes Filles en Fleur*, p. 803
17. Gregh, *Mon Amitié avec Marcel Proust*, p. 90
18. Et seq. Proust, *Correspondance Générale*, p. 135
19. De Fourcaud, p. 48
20. *Marcel Proust and his Friends*, Exhibition Catalogue, p. 12
21. *Ecrits pour l'Art*, p. VI
22. *Art et Décoration*, July-December 1911, p. 234
23. *L'Art Décoratif*, March 1905, p. 131
24. *Les Pas Effacés*, p. 296
25. *Les Roseaux Pensants*, p. 59
26. *Les Roseaux Pensants*, p. 59
27. *Les Pas Effacés*, p. 297
28. *Les Pas Effacés*, p. 298
29. Details kindly provided from family sources
30. *Ecrits pour l'Art*, p. 91
31. *Les Roseaux Pensants*, p. 58
32. Et seq. *Les Pas Effacés*, pp. 296-298
33. *Les Roseaux Pensants*, p. 59
34. Et seq. *Les Pas Effacés*, pp. 298-299
35. *Journal des Goncourt*, 15 March 1896

Chapter 8

1. *Ecrits pour l'Art*, p. 350
2. De Fourcaud, p. 45
3. De Fourcaud, p. 27
4. *Les Roseaux Pensants*, pp. 179-180
5. These words are from the poem 'Invitation au Voyage' in *Les Fleurs du Mal*
6. Private Collection, Paris
7. *Ecrits pour l'Art*, p. 215
8. Quoted in the *Ecrits pour l'Art*, p. 118
9. *Ecrits pour l'Art*, p. 215
10. Quoted in the *Ecrits pour l'Art*, p. 201
11. *Les Roseaux Pensants*, p. 180
12. *Ecrits pour l'Art*, p. 117

Bibliography

Martin Battersby, *The World of Art Nouveau*, London, 1968

Charles Baudelaire, *Les Fleurs du Mal*, Paris, 1882, *Les Curiosités Esthétiques*, Paris, 1879

Princess Bibesco, *Cahiers Marcel Proust* 2, Edit. Gallimard, Paris

Louis de Fourcaud, *Emile Gallé*, Paris, 1903

Emile Gallé, *Ecrits pour l'Art*, Paris, 1908

Fernand Gregh, *Mon Amitié avec Marcel Proust, Souvenirs et Lettres Inédites*, Paris, 1958

Edmond and Jules de Goncourt, *Journal. Mémoires de la Vie Littéraire*, Paris, 1891-96 (Vol IV)

Helga Hilschenz, *Das Glas des Jugendstils*, Düsseldorf, 1973

David Mendelson, *Le Verre, et les objets de verre dans l'univers imaginaire de Marcel Proust*, Paris, 1968

Count Robert de Montesquiou, *Les Roseaux Pensants*, Paris, 1897, *Les Pas Effacés*, Paris, 1923, *Les Chauves Souris*, Paris, 1892, *Le Chef des Odeurs Suaves*, Paris, 1893, *Les Hortensias Bleus*, Paris, 1906

George D. Painter, *Marcel Proust, A Biography*, London, 1959

Gustav Pazaurek, *Moderne Gläzer*, Leipzig, 1901

Marcel Proust, *A l'Ombre des Jeunes Filles en Fleurs, Le Côté de Guermantes*, Pléiade Edit., Paris, 1900, *Lettres et Conversations*, Edit. des Portiques, Paris, 1930, *Correspondance Générale*, Plon Edit., Paris, 1931, *Contre Ste Beuve*, Pléiade Edit., Paris, 1931

Maurice Rheims, *The Age of Art Nouveau*, London, 1960

Léon Rosenthal, *La Verrerie Française depuis Cinquante Ans*, Paris, 1927

Other sources of information consulted include the sales catalogues issued by Maître Blache, Christie, Manson & Wood, Messrs. Lair-Dubreuil & Baudoin, Sotheby & Co., *Marcel Proust and his Friends*, catalogue of an exhibition organized by Lady Jane Abdy, London, 1972, and articles in the following periodicals: *Apollo, The Architectural Record, Art et Décoration, Art et Industrie, L'Art Décoratif, The Artist, Gazette des Beaux Arts, Glass Magazine, Jardin des Arts, La Lorraine, Mercure de France, The Magazine of Art, La Nature, The Studio*.

Index

Italic figures refer to pages containing illustrations

165

60 44

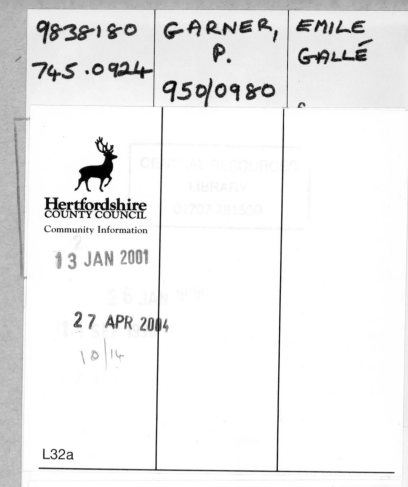